BUDGET
Right

Eliminate debt and improve your financial and mental wellbeing

CARRIE-ANN McLEAN

Imagine a life free from debt, and money in the bank. How would that feel? What could you accomplish?

It is possible! So get ready.

Budget Right will guide you to make that dream a reality, not only by eliminating debt but also improving your long-term financial and mental wellbeing.

The tools, processes and wisdom shared in this book will take you on the journey to freeing yourself from the bondage of debt - and get to the roots of misguided thinking and habits that brought you to this point.

I am living proof of the power of the process this book will take you through, from impossible debt, despair and homelessness to living a joyful life of freedom.

This book is designed to be your roadmap to your financial freedom.

My hope for you is that you achieve the financial and mental wellbeing that enables you to live the life of your dreams!

When you refuse to give up, you find a way ... this book should help you find yours.

LET'S CREATE THIS DEBT-FREE MOVEMENT TOGETHER!

Copyright © 2024 JABB Publications
Updated 2025

PO Box 1179
Carindale Qld 4152
www.jabbpublications.com.au

Instagram: @budgetrightbook
Facebook: @budgetrightbook
YouTube: @budgetright
TikTok: @budgetright
Email: hello@budgetright.com.au
Website: www.budgetright.com.au

Author: Carrie-Ann McLean

Title: Budget Right - Eliminate debt and improve your financial and mental wellbeing

PRINT ISBN: 9780645599916
EBOOK ISBN: 9780645599909
Book production: www.smartwomenpublish.com

Disclaimer

Any information in the book is purely the opinion of the author based on her personal experience and should not be taken as business or legal advice. All material is provided for educational purposes only. We recommend to always seek the advice of a qualified professional before making any decision regarding personal, financial, and business needs.

Dedication

I dedicate this book in loving memory of my dad, Robert John McLean, who encouraged me to be the best person I can be, and to never give up.

Thank you, Dad! I am the person I am today because of your gentleness and love. I miss you more than words can say, until we meet again.

To my sister, Kelley Castner, who has always been there for me and encouraged me to keep writing this book. I love you.

To those who are struggling financially, and possibly faced with homelessness – I have lived your journey, and I am sharing the path I took to take back control of my finances.

Finally, and most importantly, I dedicate this book to my Lord Jesus, who has been my rock through every struggle. He never left me, and He gave me a reason to never give up hope.

So let's not get tired of doing what is good.
At just the right time we will reap a harvest of blessing if we don't give up.

– Galatians 6:9 NLT

Contents

Foreword

In the realm of personal finance, where confusion often meets desperation, you now have a beacon of hope in your very hands, an exemplary guide on the journey toward financial freedom.

In the captivating pages ahead, Carrie generously shares not only her expertise but also her heart-warming story of triumph over crippling debt and homelessness. It is a tale that resonates deeply, reminding us all that no matter how dire our financial situations may seem, there is a way out, and there is hope.

Understanding one's spending habits is akin to peering into a mirror of truth, and Carrie is your trustworthy mirror-holder. In her compassionate exploration of mindful spending, she dismantles the myths surrounding money and urges you to embrace a mindset shift.

It's not just about what you spend money on; it's about why you spend. By delving into the intricacies of spending triggers and money mindsets, Carrie gently guides you toward the revelation that financial freedom is not merely about numbers on a balance sheet, but a holistic transformation of your relationship with money.

The journey she takes you on is not about austerity; it's about empowerment. Carrie understands that financial hardships can stem from various sources, often entwined with emotions, habits, and societal pressures. Through her insightful guidance, you'll learn to track your spending not as a tedious chore but as an act of self-care and self-discovery. You'll navigate the labyrinth of expenses, deciphering what you have committed to and what you can let go of, freeing yourself from the burden of unnecessary financial obligations.

One of the most profound lessons within these pages is the exploration of cash flow – the lifeblood of financial stability. Carrie's approach is not merely about balancing the books; it's about understanding the pulse of your finances. She empowers you to take charge, showing you how to increase your cash flow through innovative yet practical means. With her guidance, you'll learn to optimise your income streams, allowing you to not only meet your needs but also fulfill your aspirations.

Debt, that formidable adversary that haunts the dreams of many, finds its match in Carrie's expertise. Her strategies for paying off debts faster are not just about financial acumen but also about regaining control over your life. She shares proven methods that will set you on a shorter, surer path to debt freedom, liberating you from the shackles of owing, and nurturing a newfound sense of financial autonomy.

And then there are savings goals – not just dreams scribbled on wishful thinking lists but tangible, achievable targets that Carrie helps you set. Through her meticulous guidance, you'll learn the art of saving with purpose. Whether it's for that dream vacation, a home, or a comfortable retirement, Carrie's insights will transform your aspirations into actionable plans, motivating you to work steadily toward your financial ambitions.

What truly sets Carrie apart is her unwavering empathy. She has been where you are now, tangled in the web of debts and despair, and she understands the emotional toll it takes.

This book is not just a manual; it's a heartfelt offering, a guiding hand extended from someone who has emerged on the other side stronger, wiser, and more financially secure.

Her words are not just advice; they are a lifeline, a testament that no matter how dark the tunnel may seem, there is a light, and it's not just about financial abundance – it's about reclaiming your peace of mind. As you embark on this transformative odyssey through the pages of this book, do so with the knowledge that you are not alone.

You now have Carrie as your secret mentor, your confidante, and your biggest cheerleader. With her expert guidance, you can break free from the chains of debt, emerge triumphant, and bask in the radiant glow of financial freedom.

Embrace this journey. Embrace the change. Your financial freedom starts here.

Barry Nicolaou
#1 Best Selling Author & Owner at The Mindset Gap
www.barrynicolaou.com

Introduction

Do you feel like you're drowning in debt, struggling to make ends meet and unsure if you'll ever find a way out?

I know exactly how that feels. For most of my adult life, I was trapped in a cycle of debt. No matter how much my income grew, my debt grew faster, leaving me feeling miserable, anxious, and like a failure. What I was doing was obviously not working.

I wanted my life to change but didn't know where to start, because it was so overwhelming.

At the age of 49, I found myself homeless, not because of one sudden event, but as the result of years of financial mismanagement and living without a plan. I had never been taught (or learned) how to manage money, and I believed I would never achieve financial freedom or be out of debt. So, I lived accordingly.

If any of this resonates with you, know that you're not alone, and that change is possible. This book is the guide I wish I had when I felt overwhelmed and hopeless. I'll take you through my journey, sharing the lessons I learned and the tools I used to rebuild my life. From workbook pages to a budgeting spreadsheet, this book is packed with practical resources to help you create a clear, actionable plan for your own financial freedom.

This isn't a quick fix. It will take endurance, determination, patience, and a willingness to face hard truths. But if you're ready to dig deep and commit to the process, you can conquer the mountain of debt and experience the freedom and sense of accomplishment that comes with taking control of your finances

Let's start this journey together!

LET ME SHARE MY STORY WITH YOU.

Many of us were never taught how to manage money growing up. Instead, we were encouraged to get a credit card or take out a loan to buy a car as soon as we became young adults. It was all about building a good credit rating, but there was little focus on how to manage that credit or save money for the future.

My journey with debt began at seventeen with a $2,000 car loan. Over the next 29 years, it grew through multiple credit cards, personal loans, and car loans - averaging $35,000. None of it went toward investments or assets; it was all impulse spending or borrowing to pay off other debts.

I spent every dollar I earned, living for the thrill of shopping and indulging in the so-called 'good life' - night clubbing every weekend and buying whatever I wanted, whenever I wanted. Money became my escape, a way to fill the emptiness I felt inside. At the time, I didn't realise that spending was a temporary fix for the deeper issues I was struggling with.

I can now see that my spending was an attempt to fill a void, even though I hadn't yet been diagnosed with depression. It was my way of coping, but it never lasted. I struggled with depression for most of my life, but I didn't seek help until my 30s. In the meantime, I tried to buy happiness by living what I thought was the 'good life.' I spent money on things that gave me only temporary satisfaction, but instead of feeling better, I just ended up with more stress, anxiety, and depression.

Despite everything, a small part of me always wondered how things would turn out. That curiosity kept me going, even when things felt impossible. It stopped me from driving off a cliff, both literally and figuratively. In hindsight, I realise now, that what I thought was curiosity was hope.

I married at twenty-one, but the union lasted only four years. Left with nothing, I returned to Brisbane to live with my Dad and Step-Mum. Feeling like a failure in both money and relationships, I turned to alcohol, which only deepened my depression.

Alongside drinking, I also started gambling. At first, I thought it was something I could control, but it quickly spiralled into an addiction. Gambling became my way to escape the overwhelming feelings I was struggling with. But instead of helping, it only deepened my financial and emotional struggles. I thought I was in control, but the reality was, it was controlling me.

I moved to a small Queensland town in my early thirties - first to Gin Gin, then Bundaberg. It was here that I sobered up and began to see that the beliefs I had about myself (as a failure) weren't true. I discovered that I was someone who loved people and wanted to help where I could. To be the real me, I realised that I needed to be vulnerable. The beautiful community in this town showed me care and kindness, providing a safe space for me to grow.

Sobriety marked a turning point, but financial mismanagement persisted. I managed to pay off some credit cards, but I remained in significant debt. It took many years to undo the belief that I was a failure, but going through that process was necessary for me to break free from it.

I now had a new lease on life. Everything felt lighter. I still had depression and anxiety, but they did not rule me. My debt, however, was still there. I tried to manage my money better, but I didn't know how.

I sought out and read information on budgeting and money management, but despite my efforts, I struggled to put it into practice, and my budget remained nothing more than a list on paper.

In 2001, I moved back to my hometown of Brisbane to start a new career. I still didn't have my money management sorted, but I thought I was on top of it. I managed to pay off some credit cards by not using them and paying off a bit more than the minimum monthly amount. That felt good, but I still had debts of over $20,000.

Between 2001 and 2008, I thought I was doing well with my work and life, but despite my efforts, I continued to accumulate debt, including purchasing a new car, which only added to the financial strain.

In 2008, my world came crashing down when my Dad passed away at only 65 years old. My depression hit hard.

Throughout the following years my income wasn't enough to cover my bills or the lifestyle I was trying to maintain. There were times when I had to sell jewellery, furniture, and other valuables just to cover an upcoming bill. Sometimes, I used one credit card to pay off another. I lived paycheque to paycheque, without saving for emergencies or the future.

I'd consolidate my debts into one loan to lower the minimum repayments, but instead of using the extra money to pay off the debt I had just consolidated, I spent it.

At my lowest, I would panic and think that the only way out of debt was to win the lottery. So, I poured more money into gambling - not just on lotto tickets, but also scratchies, raffle tickets, bingo, art union tickets, horse racing and the pokies, all in the hope of finding a way out of debt. This addiction became out of control, which I am not proud of, but I have to be vulnerable and own up to my mistakes.

In 2012, I discovered a method to pay off debts quickly and became debt-free in 2014, which I share in detail in Chapter 11.

I became debt-free in 2014! I had learned what to do with my money and had achieved an enormous goal. I naturally thought everything would then move smoothly for me. I was wrong.

Just as I had to change my way of thinking to overcome the feeling of being a failure, the same is true with money management. You can learn the process (or as I like to say the "mechanics") of managing money, but if you don't deal with your mindset and beliefs, you will fall straight back into the debt cycle. I discuss money mindsets in Chapter 4.

I had a poverty mindset that I didn't address before I got out of debt in 2014. So, debt came back.

Here's what happened.

After I paid off my debt, I decided I wanted to study, but instead of waiting until I saved for the funds, I took out a student loan in 2014.

Then in 2016, I was looking for a career change and always had a passion to own my own business; so, I did very minimal research (bad move) and took out another loan to start a business.

I purchased a start-up online business that included training. I did learn some great things, but the promise of making $30,000 a month in sales within six months of starting the business was extremely inflated. I loved what I was doing and wanted to make it work, but I didn't have the capital to continue, so more business loans came into the picture. I was over-ambitious. Ambition isn't a bad thing, but it should be paired with wisdom.

Although the business averaged $6,000 in monthly sales, it wasn't enough to cover expenses. Not many people realise the costs of suppliers, postage, packaging, website, accounting, advertising, social media, etc. This is something I learned the hard way. By the time I recognised the extent of the problem, the business expenses and debts, including business loans and personal spending, had exceeded $150,000. With little income to pay myself, covering those debts became nearly impossible.

In May 2017, I became homeless. Thankfully, I wasn't living on the streets, but I did spend six months couch-surfing at friends' places. I'm deeply grateful for their support, knowing it wasn't easy for them either. In November 2017, I moved into a house with other friends.

From that point until 2021, I was working almost around the clock - juggling the business and taking on temporary and part-time jobs. I didn't socialise much, and once again, this took a toll on my physical and mental wellbeing. During this time, I wasn't earning enough to sustain myself, so I made the poor decision to access my superannuation.

In 2021, I sold the business for 60% less than what I originally paid to set it up. Rather than choosing bankruptcy, which had been suggested to me, I took responsibility for my debts and made the decision to pay them off. It was a tough road, but I committed to it.

To cover my living expenses, I found casual and part-time work. Once I was back on my feet, I made it a priority to shift my mindset and tackle my beliefs about money management.

In 2021, I began writing *Budget Right*, a project deeply rooted in my own experiences and lessons. My heart is in helping others see that no matter how overwhelming their current circumstances may feel, there is always hope. Change is possible. I want to show you that managing your money, breaking free from debt, and building a brighter future aren't just dreams - they are something you can achieve.

In June 2023, I returned to full-time work, and I absolutely love it. As I'm writing this, I'm thrilled to share that I'm in the final stages of paying off the last of my business debt, and (God willing) I'll be completely debt-free in 2025.

* * *

In this book, I'm not only sharing the strategy I used to pay off my debts quickly, but also the foundational money management principles I've learned along the way. Most importantly, I'll show you how to address your money mindset and beliefs.

Breaking old money habits and beliefs takes time. During your personal journey, be aware that you may start making great changes but fall back into old habits. This is part of the process. It won't always be smooth sailing; however, my greatest challenge and encouragement for you is, DON'T GIVE UP!

As I write this, I'm still in the process of paying off my debt as mentioned above. But I have a plan, and it's working. I considered waiting until I was completely debt-free before publishing this book, but I know the insights in these pages are too valuable to wait for the "perfect" time. Someone out there needs these tips, processes and skills now.

My prayer for you is that you find hope and truly believe in the goodness within yourself. Be brave, take accountability (it's a strength, not a weakness) and take action. You have the power to turn past mistakes into future triumphs. You can break free from negative money mindsets and habits, get out of debt, and live with financial freedom.

I am living proof that this process works, and I believe in your ability to take that first step toward change, no matter how hard it feels right now. Every small step forward is progress - you're not alone in this journey.

Please note, this book contains what I have learned about budgeting and money management. I am not a financial advisor, so if you need professional financial advice, please seek a reputable financial advisor. You can find them on the Tax Practitioners Board website: www.tpb.gov.au/public-register

Chapter 1

UNDERSTAND YOUR SPENDING HABITS

Do you know exactly what you are spending your money on?

With our 'tap-and-go' and 'have-it-now' culture, we have become mindless spenders.

WHY DO WE SPEND THE WAY WE DO?

Understanding your spending habits is the first step in breaking the cycle of bad money management.

Most people spend without thinking about the immediate and future costs of the purchase. Some people consider this to be impulsive spending, and they are right. However, it is also mindless spending.

Anything we do mindlessly can cost us dearly in other ways, so taking a good look at our behaviours is the starting point. You need to be honest with yourself and take responsibility for your financial situation and future money management.

Unfortunately, we now live in an 'instant society', where having to wait for things is a foreign concept. Debt spending by credit cards, loans, and buy-now-pay-later (BNPL) programs has become standard, however, normalising this way of spending has caused more harm than good.

Let's look at some recent statistics on the spending behaviours of Australians.

"In a sign of the growing pressures facing many people, Australian Bureau of Statistics data shows that for the first time since the global financial crisis,

households are spending more than they earn,

even as their homes soar in value.

He said to make up for the income shortfall,

households increased their borrowings

and were in effect 'pawning the family silver' to make ends meet."

St George Bank senior economist Pat Bustamante said during the September quarter, households spent

$1.4 billion more than they generated in income.

The last time this occurred was in the September quarter of 2008.

Source: www.smh.com.au/politics/federal/wealth-reaches-record-levels-but-households-can-t-meet-daily-bills-20231222-p5et8r.html 25 December 2023

One in four Australians, 25.1%, are finding it difficult to get by on their current income, a new analysis from The Australian National University (ANU) shows.

Source: www.anu.edu.au/news/all-news/australians-under-increasing-financial-stress

In May 2023, consumer group Choice reported the National Debt Helpline received 56,618 calls, a 29% increase on the previous 12 months.

Additionally, 94% of households told Choice their bills have increased over the previous 12 months, making the highest level of financial stress Choice has recorded in the last seven years.

Source: www.smh.com.au/money/planning-and-budgeting/financial-stress-starting-to-strain-relationships-as-cost-pressures-rise-20231115-p5ek76.html

Research shows that employee financial stress is a major workplace issue that costs Australian businesses $30.9 billion annually due to employee distraction and absenteeism.*

- Almost 1 in 2 (46%) of Australians struggle to pay for regular expenses like rent and food before payday.
- 3 in 4 Australians have difficulty budgeting for expenses each month.
- 90% of Australians have outstanding short-term debt.

*HRD Australia, 2022. A rising tide of financial stress is drowning Australia's workers.

Source: employmenthero.com/resources/australian-financial-wellness

Now is the time to break that cycle by learning a new way to manage your finances.

But first, let's look at spending behaviours.

1. Learned spending behaviour

Learned spending behaviour comes from witnessing how others around you spent money and talked about it when you were growing up. Now, don't blame your parents; they were only doing what they learned with their finances. This kind of cycle can continue through the generations – BUT this is your chance to change that now.

What did you learn about money when you were growing up? Have a good think about this, because once you recognise this, it will kick-start you to change your spending behaviour.

Here are a few questions to ask yourself about money:

- Was there always stress in the home about money?
- Were you told money does not grow on trees?
- Did you receive pocket money?
- Did you attend school excursions?
- Were you told money is evil?

- Were you shown how to save?
- Did you think money was easily accessible from a hole in the wall?
- Were you taught that money has value and how to exchange that value?
- Were you told you will never have enough money?

Take some time now to write down your thoughts and beliefs about money.

Be brutally honest and don't just think about this answer – **take action and write it down**.

We are going to discuss this further in Chapter 4.

MY THOUGHTS AND BELIEFS ABOUT MONEY

Write down your thoughts and beliefs about money on the next page. It is good to review this every few months as you will find your beliefs and attitudes towards money will change for the better over time.

My thoughts/beliefs about *money*

2. Status spending behaviour

Another reason why people spend money is for status.

A good definition of status spending is "spending money you do not have, on things you do not need, to impress people you do not like".

KEEPING UP WITH THE *Joneses*

We do not need to keep up with the Joneses or follow the crowd. Let them do their own thing, and you do what is right for you.

Think about your spending over the past five years. Are there things you have purchased just because they are or were the latest trend – or maybe you spent money to feel proud of keeping up with the in-crowd?

I'm not judging – we're all human and none of us are perfect.

Use this space to write down the things you have purchased because of status spending:

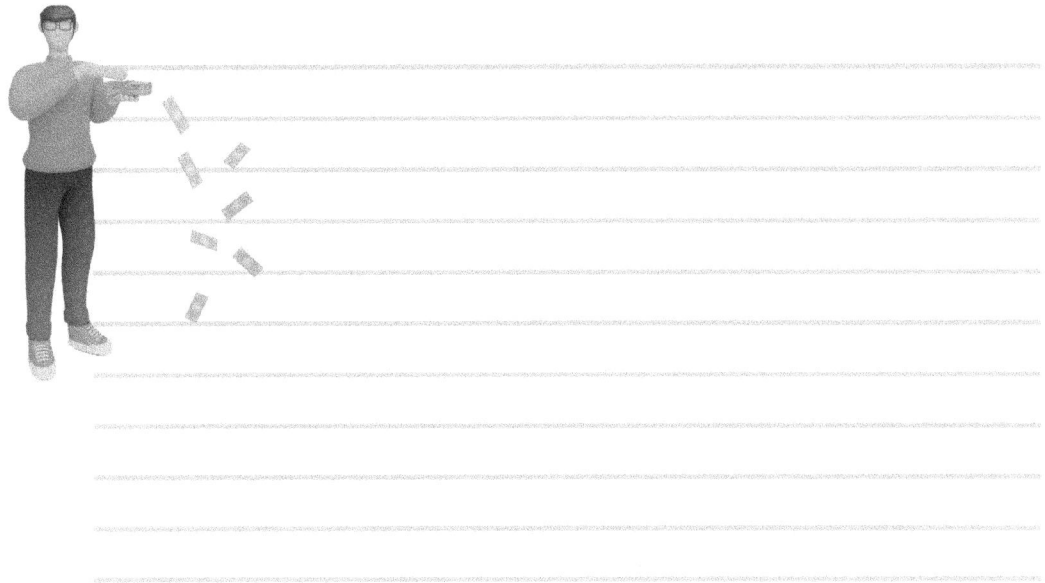

You are unique, precious and have value. You do not need to impress others. If they don't like you – it's their loss, not yours!

3. Habitual spending behaviour

Habitual or automatic spending happens when someone spends their money on products or services on automatic pilot.

What does habitual spending look like?

- Buying that morning coffee on the way to work
- Walking past the bakery and automatically going in to buy a pie
- Shopping online when bored
- Impulse spending when you walk past a sale
- Choosing a brand-name product because it's recognisable or familiar
- Spending more on your groceries because of great deals

These are just some examples: there are many more of course – but you get the idea.

These spending habits took time to develop, so it will take some time to unlearn bad habits and create new ones.

HOW LONG DOES IT TAKE TO BREAK A HABIT?

"Since the brain doesn't distinguish between good and bad habits, and it's difficult for the brain to unlearn them, it can take an average of 30 to 60 days to actually break a habit.

That's why consistency is key when trying to reach a desired goal. But when it comes to changing a habit once and for all, it can be a challenge just to start."

Source: www.mindpath.com/resource/how-long-it-takes-to-break-a-habit-and-7-steps-to-actually-do-it

Be prepared, it is going to take time to change habitual spending habits – but it can be done. And of course, I'm talking about changing from bad spending to good, wise and mindful spending habits.

WHAT ARE YOUR HABITUAL SPENDING BEHAVIOURS?

Habitual Spending

Here are some questions to prompt you to identify your habitual spending behaviours

1 Do you spend money when you are feeling sad or bored?

_____

_____

2 Do only buy a certain brand? (Clothing, food etc)

_____

_____

3 Do you buy things on sale even if you don't need them?

_____

_____

4 Do you buy a coffee on the way to work every morning?

_____

_____

5 Do you buy in bulk or stock up on things - just in case...?

_____

_____

6 Do you buy souvenirs on holidays or visiting a new place but not use them?

_____

_____

7 Do you spend a lot of money right after you get paid?

_____

_____

Record your current habitual spending behaviours. Understanding what they are will help you move forward and start to create new spending habits. You may copy this page for your own personal use.

Now it's your turn - List your habitual spending habits.

Call them out for what they are so you can tackle them head on. You cannot break a habit if you don't know what it is.

_____

_____

_____

_____

_____

_____

_____

_____

_____

_____

_____

_____

_____

_____

_____

_____

_____

_____

_____

_____

_____

_____

Break up with bad habits!

4. Addictive spending behaviour

Money spent because of an addictive behaviour could result from underlying issues that have created that behaviour.

Most people automatically think of gambling as an addictive spending behaviour; however, it can be the immediate gratification that comes from shopping.

There is an interesting article online titled "Compulsive Buying Behaviour: Clinical Comparison with Other Behavioural Addictions".

> "Compulsive buying behaviour (CBB), otherwise known as shopping addiction, pathological buying, or compulsive buying disorder, is a mental health condition characterised by the persistent, excessive, impulsive, and uncontrollable purchase of products in spite of severe psychological, social, occupational, financial consequences.
>
> Whereas ordinary non-addicted consumers state value and usefulness as their primary motives for shopping, compulsive buyers make purchases in order to improve their mood, cope with stress, gain social approval/recognition, and improve their self-image."

For the full article visit: www.ncbi.nlm.nih.gov/pmc/articles/PMC4908125

I share this with you because it is essential to call out spending behaviours for what they really are.

Learning new money management habits will help, but without dealing with any underlying challenges that cause addictive spending behaviours, it could take longer to move forward.

I have gone through this myself and can say with all honesty that real change did not stick until I dealt with my stuff.

If you do not feel comfortable speaking to your GP, here are some organisations that can help you even if you choose to remain anonymous.

It's OK to ASK for HELP

National Debt Helpline
Phone: 1800 007 007
ndh.org.au

Salvation Army
Phone: 13 72 58
salvationarmy.org.au

Beyond Blue
Phone: 1300 224 636
beyondblue.org.au

Lifeline
Phone: 13 11 14
lifeline.org.au

Australia Counselling
australiacounselling.com.au

Health Direct
healthdirect.gov.au/counsellors-and-counselling

ARE YOU READY TO MAKE A CHANGE?

A wise question to ask yourself is, *Do I want to change?*

The action you need to change starts with taking responsibility for your spending habits and financial decisions. Be wise and responsible for the stewardship over the money you have been entrusted with.

We are all on different incomes, however every single one of us needs to learn and be responsible for our own money management.

Most of us have made spending mistakes, but that does not mean we need to remain stuck there. And please do not live in the 'wish we could win lotto and make all the debt go away' mindset. Even if you won lotto, the money would be gone in no time if you have not dealt with your money mindset and spending behaviours.

So, my question to you today: Are you ready to be proactive and make changes?

Declare it now.

I, (your name) _____

choose this day (date) _____ to take

full responsibility for my own spending habits and money management. I

will make good financial decisions. I want to commit to being proactive

and mindful with my spending and money management. I will take time to

invest in myself and learn what I need to do to change wrong money thinking.

Sign: _____

Please do not feel overwhelmed by the journey you are embarking on.

It will take time to fix your current financial status and it may not go as smoothly as you hope, but by taking it day by day and step by step, this is achievable.

I highly recommend you be accountable to someone while you are on this journey. Choose someone you can trust, and who will encourage you and not judge you.

Each change you make is a step in the right direction.

If you slip back into a bad spending habit, do not be upset with yourself. We are not perfect; acknowledge it and start again.

You can do it!

Chapter 2

MINDFUL SPENDING

I am sure you have seen and heard the word *mindfulness* a lot lately. It is a powerful process and means to make a conscious effort to be aware of your thoughts, feelings, surroundings, current situation, and actions.

This sounds exhausting, right ... but do you remember when you learned to drive a car? At first, you were mindful of every action you needed to take to safely drive your car. It took time and a conscious effort to learn and understand how to start the car, when to accelerate, when to brake, how to turn a corner, etc.

It is the same with mindful spending. It will take time at first to make every single financial decision as you give careful thought and consideration to the consequences, but eventually you will be able to do this automatically.

This was once a foreign concept to me. During my darkest days of depression, asking me to make a decision, or even think about what I was thinking about was an impossible task. I know this can be tough for some people, but please persevere with this because it will benefit you, not only financially but mentally too.

Start by asking yourself these questions before you spend your money.

10 Pre-Spending Questions

Do I really need this?

How am I feeling right now?

Is this an impulse purchase?

Is this in my budget?

Will this purchase bring me closer to or further away from my big goals?

How long did I have to work to pay for this?

E.g: If I earn $25 per hour and this costs $100, I had to work 4 hours for this.

What is the real cost, are there any ongoing costs?

How often will I use this?

Am I hungry? (If you are, avoid grocery shopping.)

Is this going to increase in value?

If you ask yourself all of these questions and still make the purchase, it is also wise to ask yourself, *How am I feeling*? After you have spent your money.

After spending your money, do you feel regret, shame, or the need to hide your purchase or spending?

If you do, this could indicate a deep underlying issue with the spending behaviours we talked about in Chapter 1.

Take the time to review your spending behaviours and if you need to, please seek help by using the contact numbers provided previously.

Chapter 3

SPENDING TRIGGERS

When I learned about spending triggers, I realised that my life had been full of them. This took me a long time to deal with because I used to move my triggers around. Let me explain ...

I had been an emotional wreck most of my life and when deep emotions would flare up, I would buy a drink (normally something alcoholic – but I'm not encouraging anyone to do that as it didn't help). Once I realised drinking wasn't the answer, I began gambling at the casino, on the pokies at sporting clubs, or buying scratchy tickets and lotto. Again, after I wasted a lot of money I realised that gambling did not help: it only took my money which made me mad. Then I would buy clothes (we will talk about that later in the book) so, as you can see, I was not addressing the emotions behind the spending triggers. I was just moving them around.

You may not be in as much emotional turmoil as I once was, but I can tell you that we all have some sort of spending trigger that will push us into a spending frenzy.

Spending behaviours start with a trigger. In this chapter we are going to identify your triggers so you can put a fix in place.

IDENTIFYING SPENDING TRIGGERS

It may take you some time to identify your triggers, but the first thing to do is take pen to paper and write down your feelings and situations at the time of your recent purchases. If you can remember these over the past month, jot them down now. Can you remember what may have triggered other purchases in the past? Add them as well.

Doing this will help you identify patterns of your spending behaviour.

IDENTIFYING SPENDING TRIGGERS

PURCHASE	AMOUNT	HOW WERE YOU FEELING?

You can also use the Spending Tracking page in Chapter 5 to help you track future spending, which will also help you identify spending triggers.

Once you identify your spending triggers, you can put fixers in place to prevent yourself from unnecessary spending.

A fixer is your contingency plan for risk management. You identify the risk (your trigger) and put an action plan in place to avoid it. As you move along this journey, you will identify your triggers earlier and jump on your action plan sooner. To start with though, it may be a win-one-lose-one battle. The idea here is to keep moving forward and bringing these triggers to light. Once you are aware of them though, you can work on your battle plan.

SPENDING TRIGGER & FIXER EXAMPLES

Boredom: Being bored could be a trigger to shop online. You can put a fix in place by giving yourself a 24-to-48-hour wait time before you purchase. In most cases, by giving yourself this time and finding other things to do instead, you will realise you do not need or want that purchase.

Peer Pressure: Say your friends want you to join them on a night out, however, you know you cannot afford to go, what can you do? In these situations, you need to know your boundaries and have respect for yourself. If you struggle saying no because you do not want to upset anyone, a fix could be thanking them, but letting them know you have other plans. Your other plans could be reading a book at home. (Like this one. ☺)

Emotional: So, you have had a tough day at work and now you are tired and annoyed. Driving home, you decide to buy a take-away for dinner because you just do not want to deal with cooking. A fix could be to have some pre-made meals in the freezer. These could be leftovers or a store-bought frozen meal.

Relational: You've argued with a loved one and this triggers you to go out and spoil yourself by spending money that is not in your budget. A fix could be to go for a walk in nature, spend time with your pets, or call or visit a friend for a hug or a cry on their shoulder.

People Pleasing: You love your family and friends, so when you go out for a meal or catch up for coffee, you like to pay for everyone. This is a habit and a trigger in one. One born out of kindness. However, it does not serve you well financially to do this all the time. A fix could be either hosting a home-cooked dinner party or agreeing with everyone to pay for their own meal/coffee.

We all have spending triggers, so it is important to understand yours and put a fix in place that works for you and helps you to prevent a regretful purchase.

Now it's your turn: use the template on the next page.

SPENDING
TRIGGERS & FIXES

Spending Trigger:

My Fix:

Spending Trigger:

My Fix:

Spending Trigger:

My Fix:

Chapter 4

MONEY MINDSETS

"For as a man speaks, so is he." You may have heard this before – but what does it mean? In short – you are what you believe.

We all have beliefs about money, and these beliefs will either cause money problems or give us the power to manage money wisely.

You are what you think!

WHAT IS A POVERTY MINDSET?

Someone with this mindset believes that life is a struggle and a continuous uphill battle. They live their lives believing that making money is difficult, and they must scrimp and save everything.

This mindset will prevent you from moving forward and achieving your goals - financially, physically, and mentally.

These are common traits of someone who has a poverty mindset:

- Feels guilt as soon as they spend money
- Lacks confidence
- Constantly worries about money
- Highly critical of people who they consider as rich (judging others spending habits)
- Tends to think small rather than think big
- Learned 'poverty behaviour' from childhood
- Makes decisions based on fear

You can learn new ways of managing money and achieving your goals, but if you do not change your mindset, you will quickly fall back into the poverty mindset cycle as I did. It may take you a while, but if you fall back, don't stay there; get up and start again.

DO YOU HAVE A POVERTY MINDSET?

This was my biggest hurdle with changing my financial situation. Although I was debt free in 2014, I didn't stay that way for long because I had a poverty mindset.

I was 'poor in spirit'. This term applies when we are rooted in a victim mentality that focuses on what we don't have. It is our apparent inability to feel blessed, and we see other people as the source to meet our needs. This is a debilitating mindset, and it must be addressed for things to change.

It took me a long time to deal with this at first. I thought all I needed to do to change my situation was to start doing the right things. But those hidden beliefs and mindsets come out swinging just when you think you've got it all together.

If you find you have a poverty mindset, you may need to seek counselling or take time to invest in yourself. You will need to identify the deep root cause of your poverty mindset and learn how to move away from those thought patterns. You may want to use the journal at the back of this book to delve into your thoughts and capture them on paper.

Throughout this book, I will be showing you many ways to reduce costs and implement budgeting, however, I do not want to encourage poverty mindsets. You can be frugal but do not become miserly.

The good news is that you CAN change your mindset.

HOW TO CHANGE YOUR MONEY MINDSET FROM POVERTY TO ABUNDANCE

Begin with this simple step: Think about what you're thinking about!

Many of us let our thoughts control us, rather than us controlling our thoughts. Just because something pops in your head, it is not necessarily helpful or positive.

Over the next ten days, I ask you to make a conscious decision to listen to and journal your thoughts.

By getting into the habit of listening to your thoughts, you can quickly identify what thoughts are helping or hindering you; then you can choose which ones to act on.

As you become more aware of your thought patterns, you will be better equipped to reject thoughts that do not align with a positive money mindset.

You can do that – it is your mind.

I vote that you choose the thoughts that help you.

Here are some examples of the traits of a poverty mindset versus an abundance mindset.

ABUNDANCE MINDSET   VS   POVERTY MINDSET

ABUNDANCE MINDSET	POVERTY MINDSET
✔ Is always optomistic	✘ Thinks there is never enough
✔ "I manage my money well to be able to afford that"	✘ "I could never afford that"
✔ Is thankful & confident	✘ Is entitled & fearful
✔ Generous. Happy to share with others	✘ Sees everything as a competition
✔ Takes responsibility for their actions & decisions	✘ Sees themselves as victims
✔ Believes they have everything they need	✘ Believes they'll be happy when....
✔ Considers opportunities in situations	✘ Believes times are tough
✔ Takes control of their money management	✘ Feels anxious about money

Which one are you feeding?

There are more, but you get the drift.

If you currently have a negative money mindset, you need to change, and the best way to start is through affirmations.

Use the Money Mindset Affirmations on the next page to write your own positive statements about money.

MONEY MINDSET AFFIRMATIONS

Use this form to write your own positive money mindset affirmations to read and say out loud every day. You may copy this page for your own personal use.

Money Mindset Affirmations

Chapter 5

TRACK YOUR SPENDING

When it comes to managing your money well, you need to begin tracking your spending.

Later, in Chapter 7, we will dig deeper and talk about reconciling your bank accounts, but for now, let's concentrate on the essential step of recording your spending.

This may sound annoying because I am asking you to spend time doing this for every single purchase you make, but believe me, it is going to help you. You need to see how you are spending every dollar.

Using the next page, record your spending for the next 30 days (or longer if you prefer). You will need to copy this page for your personal use or grab yourself a notebook to keep track of your spending.

Every time you spend, you are going to record:

- the date you spent your money
- details of what you purchased or why you spent the money
- how much you spent – the exact amount
- how you paid for it – cash, credit card, buy now pay later (BNPL)
- how were you feeling – happy, sad, depressed, stressed, etc.
- how long you had to work to pay for this. Work out how many hours you need to work, based on your pay rate.

Be ruthless during this exercise. Write the information down as soon as you spend the money; do not think you will do it later, because you will forget.

This process will give you a snapshot of how you spend your money and will help you identify your spending habits.

Make sure you also include all automatic payments that are coming out of your accounts; cash purchases; credit card/BNPL (buy now pay later) purchases; loan and mortgage repayments; lay-bys, etc.

Record absolutely **everything** you are spending your money on.

You may copy this page for your own personal use.

SPENDING TRACKER

DATE	DESCRIPTION	AMOUNT	HOW PAID	HOW WAS I FEELING?	HOW LONG DO I HAVE TO WORK TO PAY FOR THIS?

Chapter 6

WHAT'S YOUR CASHFLOW?

It is a fact: you will never get ahead if you spend more than you earn.

The first step in budgeting is to take a good look at your NETT income (your take-home pay) and separate your money into four cashflow segments:

- 10% for saving
- 10% for giving or donating
- 10% for splash cash
- 70% for expenses

If you are thinking, *I cannot do this*, put that thought aside right now, because I am going to show you that you can!

You may need to work on damage control with your finances before you are able to break down your nett income into all these segments, however, this will become achievable for you.

Let's take a deeper look into these cashflow segments.

Savings Cashflow

Saving 10% of your nett income will help build your financial nest egg for retirement. You may want to save more, however 10% is a great start.

Donations Cashflow

We all want to make a difference and live in a better world, so find a reputable charity that you are passionate about and donate 10% of your nett income. Some people may give this to their church.

Splash Cash Cashflow

This is the fun one. You have worked hard for your money, so why not reward yourself with some splash cash. Treat yourself!

Expenses Cashflow

While you are working your way out of debt, allocate 70% of your nett income. This will change to 50% when you are debt free.

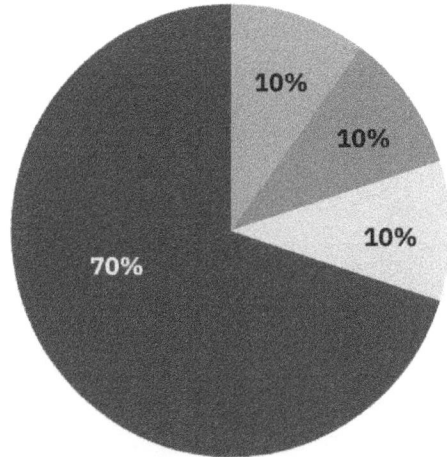

10% **10%** **10%** **70%**

SAVINGS CASHFLOW

By saving 10% of your nett income you are building your financial nest egg and making your retirement more comfortable.

This percentage is not a one-size-fits-all solution, but a good starting point. Some may need to allocate 15% or more of their nett income, however 10% is a good start.

You may be reading this book in your later years and thinking that you will not have much of a financial nest egg on 10% of your income, but I say this categorically – you will be 100% better off if you start now rather than doing nothing at all.

Here are some examples of the savings you will have each year when you put aside 10% of your nett income, which differs from one person to another.

Yearly Savings

Weekly Nett Income	10% Savings	Savings each year
$300	$30	$1560
$500	$50	$2600
$800	$80	$4160
$1000	$100	$5200
$1500	$150	$7800
$1800	$180	$9360

The total savings per year listed above do not include any interest or financial growth from investments.

As your Savings Cashflow Segment grows, seek an ethical financial advisor to guide you on the best way to invest to gain the best return.

This segment does not contain savings for goals such as a holiday or car; these savings goals will be financed from your Expenses Cashflow.

DONATIONS CASHFLOW

I am sure you have heard the saying, 'You reap what you sow'. I strongly believe in this universal rule. If you are not sowing your finances in good soil, you cannot expect a good financial harvest.

Sowing comes before a harvest. A farmer must sow seeds before their crop is ready for a yield. The same is true with our finances.

Every dollar you spend (sowing) should give you a return for your investment (reaping). For example, when you buy food, it gives you fuel for your body.

So what is your return for donating?

According to Connect Health & Community, "Giving to charities has more than monetary benefits. Donating doesn't just benefit the charity or organisation but can be rewarding for you too. Australians donate millions collectively every year to charities that support causes they believe in."

Source: connecthealth.org.au/enews/five-reasons-to-give-to-charity

Some benefits of donating to charities:

1. Makes you happier: According to Giving What We Can, "Several experimental studies have been conducted to examine whether there are any correlations between giving and level of happiness. This now backed up by MRI scans which show this 'warm-glow effect' in the reward centres of the brain."

    Source: www.givingwhatwecan.org/en-GB/get-involved/giving-and-happiness

2. Helping others can boost your heart and mind: According to the Cleveland Clinic, physical and mental health benefits associated with giving or serving can include:

    - Lower blood pressure
    - A longer lifespan
    - Less stress
    - Boosts self-esteem, elevates happiness and combats feelings of depression

    Source: health.clevelandclinic.org/why-giving-is-good-for-your-health

3.   Charities fulfil an important role in our society. They deliver vital services, respond to disasters and address a wide range of community needs. They have a unique capacity to respond to specific issues and conditions that aren't addressed by mainstream services or systems – local causes or rare conditions can find advocacy and support through a charity, often championed by individuals driven to make a difference.

Charities also represent the spirit of giving and helping – an outlet for our best intentions and a channel for our desire to reach out to others and support our communities.

Source: www.acnc.gov.au/media/news/australian-charities-report-shows-importance-sector

4.   Tax Deductable: Donations over $2 in Australia are tax deductible. This helps reduce your taxable income, which may boost your tax refund at tax time.

Source: www.ato.gov.au/individuals/income-deductions-offsets-and-records/
deductions-you-can-claim/gifts-and-donations

We all want to make a difference and live in a better world, so find a reputable charity or charities that are doing something that you are passionate about and sow 10% of your nett income as your donation cashflow.

The choice is yours.

SPLASH CASH CASHFLOW

This is the fun one. Spend 10% of your nett income on anything you want.

You have worked hard for your money, so why not reward yourself with some splash cash.

You might be asking, *Why limit my splash cash to only 10% of my nett income?*

It comes down to enjoying the things you love through discipline and a respect for money.

What can you do with your splash cash?

- Spend money on your hobbies.
- Go on that dinner date.
- Buy that outfit you've been eyeing off.
- Save for a special event.
- Use some splash cash to pay off your debts quicker.

If you are in a situation where you have excessive debt, I would recommend using some of your splash cash to pay off debts first.

Make sure you give yourself a treat though. Even if it is enjoying a coffee with a friend.

You may find something on your expense cashflow that you would like to use for splash cash cashflow, such as coffees, lunches, or spa treatments etc.

You choose your cash splash reward.

EXPENSES CASHFLOW

This may sound like an oxymoron having 'expenses' and 'cashflow' in the same title but trust me, it will make sense.

If you have financially committed to spending more than your income, it will take time to get this back under control. I will discuss expenses in further detail in Chapter 8.

The Expenses Cashflow is to cover all of your expenses.

What are expenses?

This category includes most of what you spend your money on, and is not limited to your weekly, monthly or yearly bills. The list is extensive, but here are the most common expenses:

General Expenses

- Rent/mortgage
- Electricity/gas
- Loans/credit cards/BNPL buy-now pay-later accounts
- Insurances
- Car registration/services
- Pay TV/subscriptions
- Mobile phone/Wifi
- Groceries
- Clothes
- School fees
- Medical costs
- Childcare

This is a small list, however, you will find a comprehensive list of expenses in the ©Budget Right Spreadsheet.

I have broken down expenses into 10 expense categories.

Expense Categories

GROCERIES

ENTERTAINMENT TREATS

RESIDENTIAL UTILITIES

FINANCIAL INSURANCES

PERSONAL EXPENSES

LOANS/CREDIT CARDS/BNPL

VEHICLES TRANSPORT

SAVINGS GOALS

FAMILY EXPENSES

OTHER EXPENSES

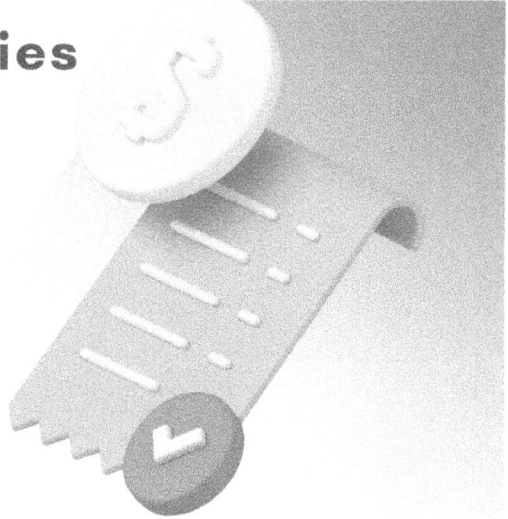

You may be surprised to find what you are spending your money on.

Chapter 7

EXPENSES – WHERE THE BUDGETING BEGINS

Without making a conscious effort to spend wisely and budget right, you could quickly lose control of your finances.

Do you really know what you have financially committed to?

Do you reconcile your bank statements? Most people do not.

Bank reconciliation is common practice in businesses; however, I encourage you to do this with your personal finances, as it will benefit you greatly. The purpose of reconciliation is to keep a track of money coming into your account (credits) and money going out of your account (debits).

By checking your bank statements regularly (I recommend you do this at least monthly), you can quickly identify any errors such as unauthorised transactions, subscriptions that were cancelled but have still been taken from your account, and discrepancies between an item's purchase and the amount you were charged.

Keep your receipts so you have proof of what you have purchased and check them against bank statements to make sure you have been charged correctly.

If there are any transactions that you do not recognise, contact your bank immediately.

Another reason to reconcile your personal accounts is to ensure you always have enough cashflow in the right accounts for your upcoming expenses. If you do not reconcile your bank statements, how do you know where your money is going?

Let me show you how to reconcile your personal accounts.

It's time to gather your bank statements covering the last three months. You may have these in print form, or you may need to login to your bank account/s and download the statements.

You most likely won't have a copy of every receipt for the past three months, so let's look at the transactions on your bank statements.

Let's make this activity fun. Grab some highlighters in six different colours.

Highlight each of the following groups of transactions in the different colours so you can easily see the types of spending appearing in your statement.

- Bank fees

- Bills

- Takeaway

- Groceries

- Entertainment

- Subscriptions

When you reconcile your bank statements every month, you may find fees, expenses or withdrawals that should not have been processed. Keep a tight rein on this. The earlier you identify these, the easier it is to fix the situation.

- Are there any transactions you don't recognise or remember?

- Are your bank fees high?

- Are there any subscriptions you thought you had cancelled, or you don't use anymore, that are still coming out of your account?

- Are there any suspicious transactions?

Starting today, make the commitment to reconcile your bank accounts every month. It may take you 30 to 60 minutes a month, but it is worth it. If you do not know what's coming out of your bank accounts, how can you truly have control over your finances?

Here is another question for you: do you know how much you have financially committed to?

Most people know they have rent or a mortgage, electricity, gas, registration, and insurances. But do you know where every single cent is being spent?

Let's work it out!

It's now time to download the ©Budget Right Spreadsheet.

To access your ©Budget Right Spreadsheet, visit this website:

https://budgetright.com.au/product/budget-right-spreadsheet/

As a reader of this book, you can download it for free using this code:
BRSPREADSHEET

If you do not have access to Microsoft Excel, you can use the **Budget Right Workbook** at the end of this book.

1. Record your nett income

Enter your nett income in the top section of the Nett Income column. Whether you are paid weekly, fortnightly or monthly, enter the amount you receive after tax, then use the dropdown box in the next column to select your pay frequency.

If there are any other income streams not listed here, use the blank spaces to enter those details.

Once you enter all your income streams and pay frequencies, it will break down your income to a weekly amount. From the weekly income, your four Cashflow Segments will automatically populate.

Your next exercise is to record all your expenses in the ©**Budget Right Spreadsheet**.

INCOME		
Income Streams	**Nett Income (After Tax)**	**Frequency Choose from List**
Weekly Wages/Salary 1	$0.00	
Weekly Wages/Salary 1	$0.00	Weekly
Rental Income	$0.00	Fortnightly
Centrelink Benefits	$0.00	Monthly
Other Income	$0.00	Quarterly
	$0.00	Yearly
	$0.00	
	$0.00	
	$0.00	
	$0.00	
Total Weekly Income	**$0.00**	
Weekly Cashflow Segments		
10% Savings Cashflow	$0.00	
10% Splash Cashflow	$0.00	
10% Donations Cashflow	$0.00	
70% Expenses Cashflow	$0.00	

2. Record your Expenses

Under the heading 'Expenses' in the ©Budget Right Spreadsheet, record how much you pay for each relevant expense, and include whether it's paid weekly, fortnightly, monthly, quarterly or yearly.

The list of expenses in the Budget Worksheet is comprehensive, however it does not include every single expense scenario. I have left room for you to add any extra expenses.

Re-visit your 21-day spending record and bank statements. Make sure you include everything you spend your money on.

I have broken down expense categories for you to work through. Each expense category has a few blank lines that you can add anything not currently included in the list. For example, you can break down your 'Groceries' expense if you shop at different specialty stores, however if you have a standard grocery budget, you can place that on one of the blank lines.

Include the amount of your expenses, and in the dropdown box in the next column, select your payment frequency.

Some expenses will increase or decrease depending on usage, such as Electricity, Gas and Water. With these expenses, record the average amount. To calculate this, add up the total years' cost for each, then either add them as a yearly expense, or divide that amount into a specific frequency. (For example, $3000 per year = $250 per month.)

Once you have entered your income and expenses, your budget breakdown will pre-populate your expense cashflow to show how much you need weekly, fortnightly or monthly.

EXPENSES		
Expense Details	**Amount**	**Frequency** Choose from List
Groceries		
Fruit & Vegetables	$0.00	
Meat, Seafood, Deli	$0.00	Weekly
Bakery	$0.00	Fortnightly
Dairy, Eggs, Fridge	$0.00	Monthly
Freezer	$0.00	Quarterly
Pantry	$0.00	Yearly
Drinks	$0.00	
Household	$0.00	
Cleaning	$0.00	
Baby	$0.00	
Pets	$0.00	
	$0.00	
	$0.00	
	$0.00	
	$0.00	
Residential/Utilities		
Rent	$0.00	
Mortgage	$0.00	
Body Corporate Fees	$0.00	

As most people are paid either weekly, fortnightly or monthly, I have set up the breakdown so you can focus on your own income frequency.

The first row, 'Total Amount Required for Expenses' will show how much you are currently spending.

BUDGET BREAKDOWN	Weekly	Fortnightly	Monthly
Total Amount Required for Expenses	$0.00	$0.00	$0.00
Your 70% Expense Cashflow Available	$0.00	$0.00	$0.00
Less Your Current Expenses	$0.00	$0.00	$0.00
Are you Under or Over Budget?	**$0.00**	**$0.00**	**$0.00**
My Budget Excess Is:	$0.00	$0.00	$0.00

The second row 'Less Your Current Expenses' is your allocated 70% Expense Cashflow budget.

Finally, the last row 'Are you Under or Over Budget' will show you if you are spending more or less than what you earn.

If you are spending more than you have allocated in you 70% Expense Cashflow, get ready to work through Damage Control in the next chapter.

If you are under budget the cashflow you have available is your **EXCESS,** which will help pay off your debts quicker.

TIP: Even if you are under budget, I highly recommend you revisit your expense budget to see what you can cut back on so you have more EXCESS to pay out your debts quicker. Do you really need everything you are spending money on?

In Chapter 11, I will share in detail the money saving options that will help you increase your **EXCESS**.

Chapter 8

DAMAGE CONTROL

If you are spending more than you earn, or struggling to make repayments on loans, credit cards or BNPL, then you need to make some tough decisions and take action through damage control.

We all have different budgets but living beyond our income is no way to live. When working your way out of debt, you may need to go without some things for a period of time.

In my experience of homelessness, I realised that all I needed was food, shelter and water.

Many of the little luxuries we call necessities are not necessities at all.

There are TWO STEPS in Damage Control.

STEP 1: REVISIT YOUR EXPENSES

What are some expenses that you can let go of or cut back?

Go through your expenses with a fine-tooth comb. You may need to go without a few things until you have your expenses under control.

As you review your expenses, ask yourself these questions. They may help you decide what to keep and what to let go of.

- Is this a necessity or a luxury?
- Is this healthy for my wellbeing?
- Will this increase in value?
- Am I getting the best price for this product/service?
- Am I paying for something I can do myself?
- Do I really need this right now?

Let's go through each expense category.

Groceries

Do you have excess food and throw some out on a weekly basis? This is a major issue. With the current cost of living crisis (in 2023), It is wise to spend your money on the food you will actually eat.

70% of the 7.6 million tonnes of food wasted in Australia every year is edible. Australian households throw away around **one in five bags of groceries**, equal to around 312kg per person.

Food waste costs the economy around $36.6 billion or $2,000 to $2,500 per household per year

Source: www.abetterchoice.com.au/choice-tips/food-waste-action-week-6-12-march-2023

Let's focus on this fact - **around one in five bags of groceries are wasted**. What does that mean to your budget? If you spend $250 per week on groceries and that comes in 5 bags - are you throwing out $50 worth of food?

How can you reduce your grocery expenses?

- Do you make meal plans? Check your weekly specials and plan your meals around those items.
- Look at what you already have in your pantry - create meals around some of those products.
- Rather than spending money on expensive pre-packaged snacks, make your own, e.g. cheese and crackers. With one box of crackers and a 250g block

of cheese, you can make five snacks for the price of one pre-packaged snack.

- If you tend to throw away a lot of fresh vegetables, buy frozen instead - and make sure you use them.

Do you have a second fridge or freezer? You really don't need to store excess food that you won't eat, and you are spending more in electricity. I will talk about this more in Chapter 9.

Here's a fun activity. Do a stocktake of all the grocery items you have in your pantry, fridge and freezer, then calculate the dollar value of your foods. You may find that the cost of this food could have been your next family holiday.

Once you have completed your Grocery Stocktake, plan meals that will use all the groceries and ingredients you currently have, before buying more groceries. This may mean having a big cook-up so you make meals and freeze them for easy weeknight dinners.

Grocery Stocktake

Date: _____

Groceries	$ Value
_____	_____
_____	_____
_____	_____
_____	_____
_____	_____
_____	_____
_____	_____
_____	_____
_____	_____
_____	_____
_____	_____
_____	_____
_____	_____
_____	_____
_____	_____
_____	_____
_____	_____
_____	_____
_____	_____
_____	_____
_____	_____
_____	_____
_____	_____
_____	_____
_____	_____
_____	_____

Residential/Utilities

Currently in 2024, the costs of rental properties and mortgages are quite high because we are in the midst of a housing crisis in most states of Australia. However, there are always things you can do to cut back and save money.

Gas and Electricity - Shop around. Are you getting the best deal? Does your property have solar? If so, use your heavy-duty appliances during the time your solar system generates the most power. Check the solar system's user manual for optimal performance.

Appliances - Check your appliances are energy efficient. You will notice in my ©Budget Right Spreadsheet that I include appliances in the budget. This is not so you can buy every new, trendy appliance, but so you have a budget in place when you need to replace your fridge or washing machine. Calculate the cost of replacement and the lifespan of your current appliance. Typically, fridges have a lifespan of 10-15 years. If your fridge is 8 years old, then calculate how much you need to save each month to replace it when it is 12 years old. (For example, if a new fridge will cost $1000 and you have 4 more years until you have to replace it, you would need to save $20.83 per month to cover the cost of that replacement.) Consider this for all your main appliances and furniture.

Pay TV and Streaming Services - Do you really need multiple streaming services or the highest Pay TV subscription? Do you need Pay TV at all? Be honest with yourself - how much TV do you watch a day, and are the costs of these services a benefit to you, or can you cut back? You should only pay for what you use, so if you need to, be ruthless and cut back.

Mobile phones - Again, shop around. Is it really important to get the latest mobile phone and lock yourself into an expensive payment plan? Look for the best deal right for you. I have seen phone plans from $15 per month but it is limited with the data, so work out exactly what you need, then compare plans.

Internet - This is normally linked to your mobile phone and/or Pay TV plans. When shopping around, check everything as it may be cheaper to have different providers for each. You can also approach your current provider, telling them the prices you have found, and ask if they can match them or improve on that cost.

Personal Expenses

Health – We need to look after our physical and mental health. This does come at a financial cost; however it does not need to break the bank.

Your health is important, so please do not put off seeing the doctor, dentist, optometrist etc. If you can find a bulk billing doctor, great. However, if not, shop around and get quotes. You can also find information on the local government websites.

Most Australians have a Medicare account which will help towards some medical expenses.

If you do not have a Medicare account, you can find details here – www.health.gov. au/topics/medicare

Check if you are eligible for a Health Care Card – www.servicesaustralia.gov.au/ health-care-card

You can get a Health Care card for up to one year if you receive any of the following government payments*:

- ABSTUDY Living Allowance
- Austudy
- JobSeeker Payment
- Parenting Payment Partnered
- Special Benefit
- Youth Allowance

*correct at the time of printing this book

There is also Private Health Insurance which can help with the cost of medical expenses. Shop around and see what is best for you. You can choose from hospital and extras, or just hospital or just extras. Work out the yearly cost of this insurance and compare that with how much you would spend on health services/products without it.

Do you have a gym membership? If so, make sure you actually use it; if not, it's time to cancel. Consider this before locking yourself into a contract – a walk does not cost anything.

Education – We never stop learning, and although we may have finished school, we should continue to invest in ourselves, and keep our mind active. You could do this by simply borrowing books that you have an interest in from your local library, or buying used copies on Amazon or other such websites. It is important to think for yourself and know what is happening around you, so keep your mind active. You may have an interest in learning a new craft or language, and you will find plenty of free YouTube videos you can utilise.

Clothing – As we don't live in a nudist society, we need clothes.

> Iconic denim brand Levi's has released new data that shows Aussies only wear 55% of what's in their wardrobe regularly, with more than half of us acknowledging that 10% of new purchases we made in the last 12 months get worn once, if at all.

Source: thelatch.com.au/how-to-recycle-clothes-sustainably

> According to Dr. Jennifer Baumgartner, clinical psychologist and author of the book 'You Are What You Wear', most Americans don a mere 20% of their closets 80% of the time. So, if you own 103 pieces of clothing (the actual average among American women), you typically wear approximately 20 of those pieces.

Source: lifelabs.design/journal/how-the-life-systems-approach-offers-less-and-more

These statistics show we do not wear everything in our wardrobe. Like you did with your groceries, take a stocktake of your wardrobe. Do you have clothes that still have the tags on them? Take everything out of your wardrobe that you have not worn in the past three months. Obviously, we need seasonal clothes, but I am talking about clothes that you just don't wear. I will talk more about this in Chapter 9.

Grooming and skincare – When I was struggling to make ends meet and was in damage control, I had to colour my own hair (yes, I could go grey and enjoy the natural beauty of it, but I like colour). Now that I have come out of that time, I can enjoy the hairdresser, however, I shopped around to find the best price for a hair colour and style. Shop around – I say that a lot, but it really does pay off.

You can also become a client at a hairdressing school salon, where trainees work on your hair under supervision, and that will be a lot cheaper than attending a regular salon.

You can treat yourself – you deserve it. If something is not in your expense cashflow budget, then save up your splash cash for your special treats. Sometimes, just going to the beach and enjoying the sun and fresh air is an amazing self-care treat.

Ok, let's talk about skincare, personal care (shampoo, etc.) and make up. How many bottles and products do you have in your bathroom? I know some people have a mini shop sitting in their bathroom cupboards. Use what you have now before you buy anything else! Just sayin'! I was very guilty of this myself and found I did not have to purchase any moisturiser for years once I did an audit on my own cupboards.

Vehicle/Transport

How many cars, motorbikes or boats do you have? If more than one, do you really need it or them? I understand families will have multiple vehicles, however if you are not using some on a weekly basis, why are you paying registration and insurance for them? Obviously, if you have a boat or caravan, you wouldn't use these weekly, however if you are not using them on a regular basis, do you really need them? They are costing you even if you are not using them. Again, I will talk about this more in Chapter 9.

Family Expenses

These expenses are unavoidable if you have a family, however you can be wise with your money in this area.

There is government support available for families, so make sure you know what assistance you can receive: go to www.qld.gov.au/families/financial/payments. If the information is confusing, set aside time and call Centrelink, or go to a local office.

If you have children at school, there are ways to cut back on expenses. If you are struggling to buy school uniforms or books, for example, you can always buy second hand.

The Smith Family is an Australian organisation that focuses on helping young Australians to overcome educational inequality caused by financial stress. They run programs and offer child sponsorship, and have staff who liaise with families. Find out more at www.thesmithfamily.com.au

Entertainment/Treat Purchases

Food – Did you know, if you spend $15 each working day (240 days per year) on coffee and lunch, it adds up to $3,600 a year? Don't get me wrong – I love coffees and a lunch out, but when you are struggling financially and have special savings goals, it pays to make your own lunches and coffees.

If you struggle knowing what to have for lunch during the week, visit your local Shopping Centre food court Sunday afternoons from 3 pm. Many food outlets offer meal deals at great prices, and you can freeze them for later in the week.

You can also make your own sandwiches or salads to take to work; and buy yourself a keep-cup/coffee flask and make your own coffees.

I will say that many coffee shops and food businesses were hit hard during the Covid lockdowns, so they do need our support. When in damage control, you will need to cut back on this, however you can use your splash cash or choose one day a week or fortnight to treat yourself to coffee and lunch.

Entertainment – I absolutely love the theatre and concerts; however, they can be expensive. My sister and I attend local theatre groups a couple of times a year now, but when I couldn't afford to go to any of these, I used the radio as my 'concert' and danced around the house. I watched movies on my TV for my theatre-fix; and occasionally I would go to the city and sit and watch people, and make up my own stories about their lives - all pleasant of course, and very entertaining.

Gift giving – I used to struggle with this because giving gifts is one of my love languages, so I would go crazy and spend debt money on them. Gift-giving on a budget can come in a variety of ways. It's often about thinking outside the box and does not have to have a financial element. For example, time is a valuable commodity so spending quality time is a gift in and of itself.

I have included alcohol, cigarettes and gambling in this section. My Dad died from lung cancer so I guess you can imagine my thoughts on smoking. I had alcohol and gambling addictions, and I know the physical, mental and financial cost that this caused. To be clear, there is no judgement on these; all I ask is that you consider the financial impact on your budget, and your life.

Financial/Insurances

Today there is insurance for everything – home, car, life, health, pets, alien abduction, and more. Yes, there are some crazy insurances. What do we really need?

As I have stated earlier, I am not a financial adviser. You should seek a reputable financial advisor, but at the very least you can ask yourself these questions.

- What am I covered for?
- How does this coverage compare with similar products on the market?
- Do I need this level of cover, or could I potentially amend at a lesser value?
- What is the excess?
- Are there payment options?

Whatever you do, be prepared to shop around!

Loans/Credit Cards/BNPL

Because this book is about financial freedom where you manage your money without the use of loans, credit cards, and buy-now pay-later plans, I encourage you to pay off these debts ASAP. Then cut up the credit cards and close your BNPL account/s. I will discuss this topic in more detail in Chapter 11.

Savings Goals

Growing your savings begins with creating a savings mindset. A simple goal of saving at least $5.00 a week can help you create a savings habit. Keep your eye on the prize. As you progress, consider the things you want to save for. A holiday, a weekend getaway, renovating, a new car.

I share more on saving goals in Chapter 12.

Other Expenses

What else are you spending your money on? Think about whether you really need it, and if you do, are you getting the best deal for it?

*　*　*

Now that you have used the above hints to revise your expenses, what is your new **EXCESS** in your spreadsheet? You are going to use this **EXCESS** to pay off your debts quicker. I will show you how in Chapter 11.

STEP 2: SEEK HELP

Let me be very clear – once you have revised your budget expenses by cutting back on everything you can, seeking help is proactive.

Many people feel ashamed and embarrassed to admit they need to seek help. I spent many years living with shame, and it got me nowhere. So, please – with all my heart, I encourage you to be brave, and take the following steps:

1. Contact your creditors

Contact your creditors (the businesses you owe money to) because communication is key. When creditors know their customers are struggling financially, they are often keen to work towards a solution. You may need to work with them on a payment plan or financial hardship agreement.

Honesty is the best policy. Do not avoid the tough conversations. Avoidance creates anxiety and this could snowball into emotional, physical or mental stress.

2. Consolidate your debts

If you have multiple credit cards and/or loans, you may be able to consolidate your debts into one manageable loan.

I caution you to take this step carefully. If you are consolidating debts, check the fine print. Are you able to pay out the loan without any penalties? I do not want to encourage more debt, so if you are consolidating, cancel all your credit cards/BNPL and other loans so you do not increase your debt.

When consolidating debts, your monthly repayments will be smaller than the total of the individual debt repayments. I will talk more on this in Chapter 11.

3. Seek financial counselling or talk to your GP

Financial stress can be debilitating to your physical, emotional and mental wellbeing. In Chapter 1, I provided information about organisations you can contact to seek counselling.

4. Increase your cashflow

There are many ways to increase your cashflow, which I discuss further in Chapter 9.

Increasing cashflow is achievable for everyone, however, it may only be a temporary fix to help you pay off some of your debts.

With every opportunity to increase your cashflow, it will require you to be proactive in either letting go of stuff or using your talents or assets.

You may increase your cashflow by $100 or $10,000, or more; but whatever the amount, use it wisely to pay off your debts. **Do not increase your spending**.

5. Contact charity support

If you are in a real crisis, there are charities and churches that can provide food parcels. They can also support you emotionally during this time.

When you are on the other side of this debt, it is a wonderful thing to give back to these charities so they can continue to help others who are going through the same thing you did.

Chapter 9

INCREASE YOUR CASHFLOW

There are numerous ways to increase your cashflow. Let's focus on a few small things you may be able to do now.

YOUR 'STUFF'

Did you realise that your next holiday could be sitting in your wardrobe, cupboards or garage?

What do you have lying around the house that you never use?

If you do not use it or wear it, and it has no sentimental value and it is in good condition, sell it. Here are some suggestions of the stuff you could sell.

Sell your Stuff

- [x] Clothes, Shoes & Accessories
- [x] White Goods (Fridge, Freezers)
- [x] Cookware
- [x] Collectables
- [x] Fine Jewellery
- [x] Toys
- [x] Vinyl LP Records, Cassette Tapes
- [x] Musical Instruments
- [x] Books
- [x] Lawn & Garden Tools
- [x] Art, Prints, Paintings
- [x] Sporting Goods
- [x] Sewing Machine, Craft Products/Tools
- [x] Camping/Fishing Equipment
- [x] Mobile Phone, Tablets, Computers
- [x] Furniture
- [x] Electrical Items – TVs, Air Fryer, Juicers etc
- [x] Tupperware
- [x] Lego
- [x] Exercise Equipment
- [x] DVDs, Videos
- [x] Baby Clothes, Furniture & Equipment
- [x] Cars, Car Parts, Boats, Motorbikes, Caravans
- [x] Crystal, Vintage Dishes, Glassware

You might be surprised at how much cashflow you have sitting in your stuff.

There are so many ways to sell your stuff. You could have a garage sale; sell it through online platforms such as Facebook Marketplace, Gumtree or eBay; or sell to pawn shops.

Do your homework. You may have some things of great value, so search what is currently for sale, and compare prices.

If you are selling items through online platforms, take good photos and write details of the product, giving as much information as possible. Know the price you will accept, as many people will barter. Be cautious of who you are selling to. Unfortunately, there are people out there who scam. All I will say is do not accept payments by PAYID or PayPal transfers, and if on Facebook Marketplace, check the buyers' profiles.

YOUR SKILLS

We all have something we're good at. If you think you are not good at anything, that's a lie.

You do have skills – you just may not know it. How do you find out?

- Write a list of what you love doing and what you are passionate about it.
- Ask your family and friends what they think you are good at.

You will soon discover what your skills are. Turning your skills into extra income is an effective way to increase your cashflow.

- Sell your baking/cooking or craft products (at markets, to retailers, through online sale platforms).
- Teach your skill to others (run classes, write a course, be a tutor).
- Do freelance work (write resumés for people seeking work; create social media posts for small business owners; research and write blogs for others; do IT work; do SEO work on websites, etc.).
- Provide companionship or home care, etc.
- Provide pet sitting or dog walking services.
- Advertise your services online through freelance platforms such as Airtasker, Fiverr, Upwork, etc. These could include house cleaning, lawn/pool maintenance, ironing, courier services, social media, administrative virtual assistant.
- Write a book or start a blog that may eventually earn income.

HOW MUCH CAN YOU EARN?

Gardening Jobs	Cleaning Jobs	Delivery Jobs	Assembly Jobs
$170-$310	**$150-$300**	**$80-$120**	**$150-$160**

Source: Airtasker

USE YOUR ASSETS

TO INCREASE YOUR CASHFLOW

What assets do you have right now?

You can make money from your current assists such as:

- Spare room
- Unused garage or shed
- Mower & gardening equipment
- Cleaning products
- Car
- Boat

How can these help you earn extra money?

- Rent out your spare room either as an Airbnb or a 6-12 month tenancy.
- Rent your unused garage or shed to someone needing storage space, or convert it to a residential rental room (check council regulations first).
- Offer house cleaning and/or lawn and garden maintenance.
- Offer car cleaning/detailing.
- Use your car for extra income. Sign up to ride share companies such as Uber, Didi, Ola etc.
- Rent out your boat (www.bookmyboat.com.au)

There are many more ways to increase your cashflow, however these are great places to start.

In my darkest days of depression, I could not handle doing anything extra, so be kind to yourself if you are going through those times. Take one day at a time.

Chapter 10

BANK ACCOUNTS

When you break down your budget, I recommend you open several bank accounts so you can separate your money for use in your different cashflow segments.

EVERYDAY ACCOUNT

This is the account that your pay will be deposited into, and the base from which you transfer all your cashflow segment allocations into their relevant bank accounts.

You can keep your splash cash segment in this account or withdraw the cash for your splash cash fun.

BILLS/EXPENSE ACCOUNT

Open an account with a visa debit card attached, so you can pay your bills directly from this account through BPay or direct debit. Using the ©Budget Right Spreadsheet, you will see how much you need weekly, fortnightly and monthly to allocate to your expenses. From your pay, transfer that amount into your Bills/Expense Account.

This will ensure the funds are available when the bills are due.

If you want to batch (or separate) your bills, you can open multiple Bills/Expense Accounts. You may want to have different bill accounts for your home expenses, your car expenses, or your family expenses.

Bank Accounts

Everyday Account

This is the account that your pay will be deposited into, and the base from which you transfer all your cashflow quadrant allocations into their relevant bank accounts.

Bills/Expense Account

Open an account with a visa debit card attached, so you can pay your bills directly from this account through BPay or direct debit. From your pay, transfer that amount into your Bills/Expense Account.

Savings Account

For each savings goal you have, open a high-interest sub account. When you work out what you want to save for, you need to calculate the full amount you require, and timeframe you need to save enough money.

Emergency Account

Open a high-interest savings account for emergencies only. I recommend having a minimum amount of $2,000 in this account, however it would be ideal to have three to six months of your nett income saved in this account.

Investment/Savings Account

This is from your 10% Savings Cashflow Quadrant. You can open a high-interest account to start building for your retirement and nest egg.

SAVINGS ACCOUNT

(for savings goals from your expense cashflow)

What do you want to save for?

Do you want to buy a new car, go on a holiday or save for a wedding?

For each savings goal you have, open a high-interest sub account.

When you work out what you want to save for, you need to calculate the full amount you require, and timeframe you need to save enough money.

We will go into more detail in Chapter 12.

EMERGENCY ACCOUNT

Open a high-interest savings account for emergencies only. I recommend having a minimum amount of $2,000 in this account, however it would be ideal to have three to six months of your nett income saved in this account.

This is for those unexpected situations like urgent home repairs or illness.

You may not have $2000 to deposit into this emergency account right away, so start with depositing at least 2% to 5% of your nett income until your emergency account has a minimum of $2000, or the value of three to six months' expenses. You can add this to your expense cashflow segment while you are building up this account.

Set up an automatic transfer into your Emergency Account for each pay period (i.e.: weekly, fortnightly, monthly).

INVESTMENT/SAVINGS ACCOUNT

(This is from your 10% Savings Cashflow Segment)

This is where I recommend you also seek professional advice through an ethical financial advisor.

To begin with though, you can open a high-interest account to start building for your retirement and nest egg.

You may be thinking that's what your superannuation is for. However, having excess finances at your discretion is a huge advantage if the need arises.

Chapter 11

PAY OFF DEBTS QUICKER

Debt can be crippling and overwhelming, so it is important to take action to pay them off quickly.

Let me ask you a few questions:

Have you ever received a pay rise?
Have you paid off a credit card in the past?
Have you sold some of your stuff?

If you answered yes to any of these questions, where did the money go?

Let me guess – about 90% of you will say *I don't know*.

Well, now it's time for you to become aware, know where your money goes, and actively use that money to get rid of your debt.

Firstly, let me point out some facts about credit cards and BNPL.

Credit Cards

Did you know that if you are only paying the minimum amount each month on your credit card, it will take you on average **5 years and 2 months to pay off each individual credit card**. That is, if you don't increase the current credit balance in that time.

CREDIT CARD STATISTICS

18-35	43% have 1 card 21% have 2 cards 6% have 3+ cards

35-54	45% have 1 card 20% have 2 cards 8% have 3+ cards

55+	47% have 1 card 20% have 2 cards 7% have 3+ cards

According to Finder's latest Consumer Sentiment Tracker data, 68% of Australians say they have a credit card, with younger generations slightly more likely to have additional cards.

https://www.finder.com.au/credit-cards/credit-card-statistics

Buy Now Pay Later (BNPL)

Since the BNPL payment options were introduced in the 2010s, it has exploded as a popular payment option for millions of Australians. This option is sold to you as a no-fee option, however, if you miss payments there are fees, and it does affect your credit rating.

Also consider the cost to the businesses who offer these payment options. Our small business owners are already struggling to make their businesses profitable.

"Merchants pay anywhere from 2% to 8% merchant service fees on BNPL transactions, well above the 1.25-1.5% credit card transaction fees paid by SMEs."

Source: www.grantthornton.com.au/insights/blogs/true-cost-buy-now-pay-later

Note: For every $10,000 in credit card/BNPL account limit, your real estate borrowing power is reduced by $55,000.

Source: www.liberty.com.au/blog/loan-school/how-credit-cards-lower-your-loan-amount

DEBT REDUCTION FORMULA USING YOUR EXCESS

Now it is time to learn how to use your **EXCESS** to pay off your debts quicker.

Now that you have revised your expense budget back in Chapter 8, use the Budget Breakdown section on the ©Budget Right Spreadsheet to work out your monthly **EXCESS**.

BUDGET BREAKDOWN	Weekly	Fortnightly	Monthly
Total Amount Required for Expenses	$0.00	$0.00	$0.00

	Weekly	Fortnightly	Monthly
Your 70% Expense Cashflow Available	$0.00	$0.00	$0.00
Less Your Current Expenses	$0.00	$0.00	$0.00
Are you Under or Over Budget?	**$0.00**	**$0.00**	**$0.00**
My Budget Excess is:	$0.00	$0.00	$0.00

My monthly **EXCESS** is $_____

By shopping around and letting go of things they do not need, most people can find anywhere between $300 to $700 per month. Whatever your **EXCESS** is, this will help you pay off your debts quicker.

You are also going to use the money you make from selling your stuff, and the money generated from the other ways you have increased your cashflow.

If you have a garage sale and make $1,000, pay that money directly on the smallest debt you owe. Do this whenever you sell something or receive extra money. The goal is to pay off your debt.

You are now going to use your **EXCESS** to pay off your debts quicker.

1. Write down all your debts with the current balance owing and your minimum monthly payment.
2. Starting with your smallest debt, add your **EXCESS** to the minimum monthly payment and pay that amount until you pay off that debt.

Once you have paid off each credit card and BNPL account – cut up the cards and close your BNPL accounts! Enjoy cutting up the card/s as a symbol of your debt-free life. Don't let them control and trap you anymore.

You will continue to pay the minimum monthly payments on your other debts while you are smashing out each one – smallest to highest.

Once you have paid off one debt, add the previous Monthly **EXCESS** + Minimum Monthly Payment to your next minimum monthly payment.

In the scenario below, the total debt of $9,700 would be paid off in 14 months.

EXCESS *Debt Reduction*

DEBT TYPE	BALANCE DUE	MIN MONTHLY PAYMENT	CURRENT EXCESS	*MIN MONTHLY + MONTHLY EXCESS	WILL BE PAID OFF IN # OF MONTHS
CREDIT CARD	$500.00	$20.00	$500.00	$520.00	1 MONTH
BNPL	$1,000.00	$20.00	$520.00	$540.00	2 MONTHS
CREDIT CARD	$1,200.00	$45.00	$540.00	$585.00	2 MONTHS
CREDIT CARD	$2,000.00	$75.00	$585.00	$660.00	3 MONTHS
PERSONAL LOAN	$5,000.00	$100.00	$660.00	$760.00	6 MONTHS

While you are paying off each debt with your **EXCESS**, keep making the minimum payments on your other debts until you have cleared the previous debts.

Once you have paid off your credit card, BNPL and personal loans, it's time to pay off your next debts using the same process above.

For example, if you have a car loan at $550 per month, and now added the Monthly **EXCESS** + Minimum Monthly Payment of $760 to those payments, you could repay $1310.00 per month. If you had $18,000 remaining on your car loan, you would pay it off in under 14 months.

You can then use this same process to pay off your mortgage.

You may be thinking, *I cannot find $500 **EXCESS** per month* - that's ok. As long as you have really cut back on non-essentials, you will still have some **EXCESS** and it will help you to reduce your debt quicker than you thought possible. Also, if you have sold some items around the house, you will use that money towards paying off your smallest debt.

Now It's your turn. Write down all your debts starting with the smallest amount owing.

EXCESS *Debt Reduction*

DEBT TYPE	BALANCE DUE	MIN MONTHLY PAYMENT	CURRENT EXCESS	MIN MONTHLY + MONTHLY EXCESS	WILL BE PAID OFF IN # OF MONTHS

Imagine what it would feel like to have no credit card, BNPL or personal loan debt. It is possible!

DEBT REDUCTION TRACKER

It's encouraging to see your progress visually. You may print this page for your own individual use. Use this form for each individual debt or your overall debt. Give yourself little rewards along the way. You deserve it.

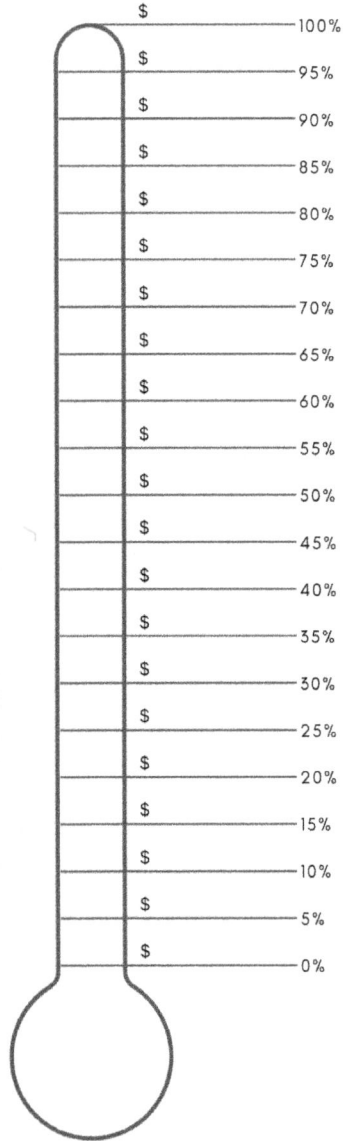

Amount Due

$_____

Notes:

$ 100%
$ 95%
$ 90%
$ 85%
$ 80%
$ 75%
$ 70%
$ 65%
$ 60%
$ 55%
$ 50%
$ 45%
$ 40%
$ 35%
$ 30%
$ 25%
$ 20%
$ 15%
$ 10%
$ 5%
$ 0%

Chapter 12

SAVINGS GOALS

To get what you want, you need to save for it. This takes time and planning.

Instead of using debt, consider being patient, and set yourself a savings goal for your desired **THING**. You will be surprised at the feeling of joy that comes from achieving savings goals and purchasing **THINGS** with your own money.

When setting savings goals, you need to consider all of the costs.

For example, there is more than the cost of the plane ticket if you are saving for a holiday, and there's a list of ongoing costs if you are saving for a car.

What do you want to save for?

- Holiday
- Home (Real Estate)
- Car, Boat, Motorbike, Caravan
- Wedding
- Starting a Business
- Furniture
- Emergency Account (3 to 6 months income)

Aside from considering all the costs, you must also consider the time frame you need to save the amount you require. This will help you identify how much you need to set aside from each pay.

For example, if you want to have a holiday in 10 months, and your total cost is $5,000, you will need to allocate $500 per month (or $125 per week).

You can have multiple saving goals. They may be long term or short term, however whatever you are saving for, you can use the Savings Goal Planner at the end of this chapter for each one.

For each of your savings goals, I suggest you open a high-interest sub account so you can keep track of each one, and ensure you are using those funds purely for the relevant savings goal.

You will have noticed in Chapter 7, I included Savings Goals in your expense cashflow segment. Your savings goals need to come from your 70% expenses cashflow and not from the 10% savings cashflow, as that is for your retirement and building your financial nest egg.

Here are some examples of costs you may want to consider.

HOLIDAY COSTS

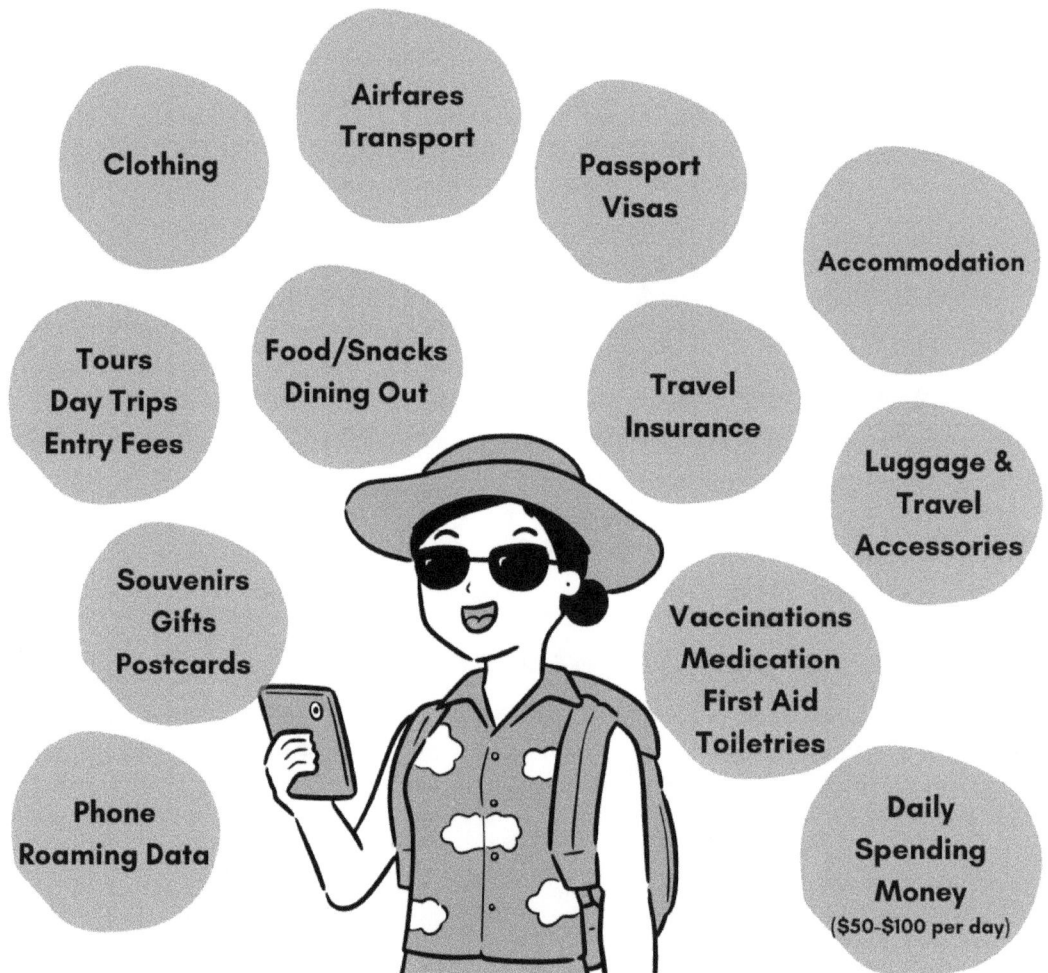

Clothing

Airfares
Transport

Passport
Visas

Accommodation

Tours
Day Trips
Entry Fees

Food/Snacks
Dining Out

Travel
Insurance

Luggage &
Travel
Accessories

Souvenirs
Gifts
Postcards

Vaccinations
Medication
First Aid
Toiletries

Phone
Roaming Data

Daily
Spending
Money
($50–$100 per day)

CAR COSTS

- ☑ **Price of the Car**
- ☑ **Registration**
- ☑ **Car Insurance**
- ☑ **Roadworthy/Vehicle Check**
- ☑ **Car Accessories**
- ☑ **Fuel**
- ☑ **Servicing**
- ☑ **Tyres**
- ☑ **Roadside Assist**

HOUSE COSTS

FOR SALE

Also consider how much you need to save for a house deposit. On average it's 20% of the cost of the property.

- ✓ Price of House/Unit
- ✓ Conveyancing
- ✓ Building & Pest Inspection
- ✓ Home & Contents Insurance
- ✓ Interest Rates & Repayments
- ✓ Maintenance
- ✓ Electricity
- ✓ Gas
- ✓ Rates
- ✓ Body Corporate (if required)
- ✓ Appliances
- ✓ Furniture

You may print this page for your own individual use.

SAVINGS GOAL PLANNER

GOAL AMOUNT:	START DATE:	DUE DATE:

GOAL DESCRIPTION:

GOAL PROGRESS: 0%   ☐☐☐☐☐☐☐☐☐☐   100%

HOW MUCH TO SAVE:	PER WEEK / FORTNIGHT / MONTHLY

ALL COSTS

DETAILS	AMOUNT

NOTES:

Chapter 13

COST SAVING TIPS

There are many ways to save money. We are going to look at just some of these, however once you start thinking about saving money, you will find plenty of opportunities.

Each day we can make small changes in our shopping behaviour that will save money each week.

When purchasing any discount offers, only purchase what you actually need. You won't be saving anything if you buy just because it's on sale.

HOUSEHOLD

Utility Costs

So, how much is standby mode costing you?

Standby power can be responsible for up to 10% of your energy bill, according to Energy Australia. And, with energy prices rising by up to 25% as of July 1. A recent survey by Finder also found the average quarterly energy bill hit a record high of $408 in September.

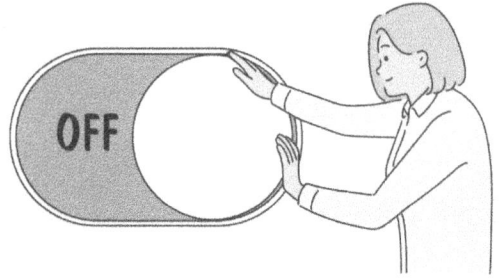

Source: https://au.finance.yahoo.com/news/will-turning-appliances-off-at-the-powerpoint-save-me-money-230358986.html

With the stats above, you could save $40 per quarter, just by turning off standby. Everything listed below will help save money. The amounts will vary.

- ✓ Stop using the dryer and hang clothes on the clothesline or air dryer.

- ✓ Always wash in cold water.

- ✓ Turn the power off at the powerpoint. Do not leave stand-by on.

- ✓ Turn lights off if you are not using them.

- ✓ Replace old washing machines, or other appliances that use more energy, with energy-efficient appliances.

- ✓ When boiling the kettle, only heat the amount of water you need.

- ✓ Use energy-efficient light bulbs.

- ✓ Where possible, avoid using the air-conditioner. If you do need to use it, keep it on 24 degrees and turn it off when you are not in the room.

- ✓ Dress for the temperature. In winter, wear jumpers and warm socks or rug up in a blanket instead of using the heater. In summer, wear cool clothes, open the windows and if it's really hot, I like to put my feet in a bucket of cold water.

- ✓ Sell the second fridge or freezer. You could get anywhere between $100 to $500 or more depending on the age, brand and condition of the fridge. I'd recommend paying this on your lowest debt.

Subscriptions

Do you really need TV/streaming subscriptions? If so, only keep one: you do not need multiple.

The average Australian household pays $50 per month for their streaming service(s), which works out to be $600 per year. The 18-29 year old bracket were spending the least amount on streaming services ($43 per month), while the 30 to 39 year old and 40 to 49 year old brackets were spending the most ($55 and $54 per month respectively).

Source: www.canstarblue.com.au/streaming/average-video-streaming-cost

Looking at these prices, is $600 per year worth it? Consider these costs carefully. I am not saying you cannot have these, however be wise with your subscriptions.

- Compare prices for your electricity, gas, telephone (landline and/or mobile) and wi-fi.
- Cancel all subscriptions you do not use (or need).

Furniture/White Goods/Electrical

✓ You can find good quality furniture at op shops, garage sales and online platforms such as Facebook Marketplace, Gumtree and eBay. For any electrical products, make sure they have been checked and tagged so they are safe for use.

✓ Look for local warehouse outlets where you can purchase new furniture, white goods and electrical products at a discounted price.

✓ You do not need top brand names when you are working your way out of debt: shop for necessity and shop around for the best price.

Laundry Savings

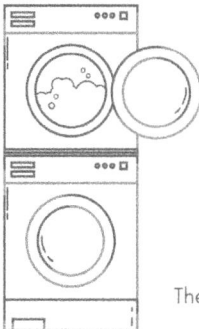

Use Cold Water

7 Loads per week using hot water costs $46 yearly

Avoid Dryer

Using the Dryer 6 times per week costs $360 yearly

These 2 simple changes could save you **$406** each year

What are the costs per year?

1 Coffee per day (average cost $5.50)	Lunch 5 days per week (average $20 per day, 48 weeks per year)	1 Pedi & Mani every 3 weeks (average cost $120)	Lotto and Scratchie Tickets (average spend $25 per week)
$2007	$4800	$2080	$1300

*Prices above are calculated on average costs.

Groceries

✓ Check your local supermarkets, bakeries, butchers, and fruit and vegetable stores for their latest specials, and menu plan around those specials.

✓ Use a shopping list and stick to it. Shop online for your groceries with click-and-collect. It will avoid impulse spending at the supermarket.

✓ Do not go shopping when you are hungry or thirsty.

✓ Do you throw out food because it is out-of-date or going off? Buy frozen vegetables and buy only what you need.

✓ Do not buy bottled water. If you cannot drink tap water, use filter jugs, filter systems, or re-fill large water bottles (e.g.: 10-15 litres) from water dispensers.

✓ If you are in dire straits, there are many places that offer free or discounted groceries such as Foodbank, churches and Lighthouse Care. Search 'Grocery help near me' to find your local support service.

✓ Start a backyard vegie patch. Grow your favourite fruit, vegetables, and herbs.

Vehicle Expenses

- ✓ Never let your petrol/fuel get below half full: fill up at 'half time'.

- ✓ Get your vehicle serviced regularly – shop around for a reputable mechanic.

- ✓ Check oil and water weekly.

- ✓ Check your tyre pressure. (Under-inflated tyres increase your vehicle's drag, which increases fuel consumption.)

- ✓ Sign up to petrol reward programs and use grocery fuel vouchers. At the time of writing this book, there's a 7/11 fuel app where you can lock in cheaper prices; Freedom Fuels has a Family and Friends membership offering of at least 6 cents, and up to 13 cents per litre discount; and the major grocery stores have 4 cents off per litre with purchases over $30.

Clothing

- ✓ Good quality clothing, shoes and accessories can be purchased at op shops, garage sales and online platforms such as Facebook Marketplace, Gumtree and eBay.

- ✓ There are many outlet shopping centres with brand new clothing, shoes and accessories at a discounted price.

DINING OUT

- ✓ Instead of meetings friends at restaurants for dinner, do the old-fashioned thing and invite them to your place for dinner for a home-cooked meal.

- ✓ If you do want to dine out, look for restaurants that have a happy-hour deal with cheaper meals if you eat early in the evening, or on quieter evenings during the week, like Mondays and Tuesdays.

- ✓ Sign up to your favourite restaurants for reward offers. They may have birthday offers, specials and freebies.

Things to consider

- ✓ Be aware of ATM fees. If you need to withdraw cash, use your own bank's ATMs, so you are not charged withdrawal fees. There are also some stores that will allow you to withdraw cash at the checkout without incurring fees, such as Coles and Woolworths.

- ✓ Do not save credit card details online. This is not only for security reasons, but it also prevents instant purchases. (Better still – cancel all your credit cards!)

- ✓ If purchasing online, be aware of the delivery fees, and if purchasing overseas, consider the currency exchange rate and fees.

SHOP AROUND / COMPARE PRICES!

Are you getting the best deal on your insurances, phone, electricity, gas, etc.?

There are so many businesses and service providers available, it is beneficial to take the time to shop around for a better deal.

If you have been a long-time customer with a specific provider, contact them and ask about a better deal they can offer.

It may take time, but it's worth it if it saves you hundreds, or even thousands, of dollars per year.

Do not automatically renew insurances. When renewals come up, take that time to shop around.

Shop around for the best price and deals on everything.

- Groceries
- Clothing
- Hair & beauty
- Holidays
- Fuel

SWAP & SAVE
Possible Annual Savings

Mobile Phone Plan	$141
Electricity	$244
Gas	$221
Health Insurance	$251
Home and Contents Insurance	$797
Car Insurance	$834

Total Savings
$2,488

Canstar. Average to Lowest/5 Star Average

EVERYONE LOVES A FREEBIE

✓ Check your bank for cashback and rebate offers.

✓ Check loyalty rewards (make the most of them to work for you) - Frequent Flyers, Flybuys, health funds, RACQ, etc. They all have member benefits.

✓ Many of your favourite businesses offer birthday rewards when you subscribe to their emails. Consider creating a special email address just for these subscription emails.

✓ Once a year, many councils have a kerbside large-item collection where homeowners place furniture and household items on their footpath. During this time, you can search your local area for attractive and useful free items.

However, please be considerate of those providing free offers. When you subscribe to businesses for freebies, make sure you support them by purchasing from them. Don't just take - become a loyal customer so they can continue their business.

*   *   *

As you can see there are many ways to save costs. Once you start looking for ways to save, you will be consciously aware of other opportunities to identify and save money you are spending on things you do not need.

I love this quote from Henry David Thoreau - "He who buys what he does not need, steals from himself".

Now it's time to put what you have learned into action.

The following section of this book contains the Budget Right Workbook Pages where you can manually work on your budget.

Alternatively, you can use the pre-formulated ©Budget Right Spreadsheet.

You can access this on my website - www.budgetright.com.au/product/budget-right-spreadsheet

Use code BRSPREADSHEET to get it for FREE!

BUDGET *Right*

WORKBOOK PAGES

For the purpose of this budget workbook, we will work on a weekly budget. You will manually need to adjust each amount.

First, we will start with your income streams.

Whether you are paid weekly, fortnightly or monthly, please calculate each income stream to a weekly payment.

Fortnightly income streams need to be multiplied by 26 then divided by 52.

Monthly income streams need to be divided by 52.

Next is to divide your income streams into your four Cashflow Segments.

Once you have added your total weekly Income Steams, work out the percentages for each Weekly Cashflow Segments.

Next, we will dive deep into your expenses.

I have broken the Expenses into nine expense categories. There is a list of expenses and some blank spaces for you to add other expenses. When you have completed each expense category, add the expenses to give you a total for that category.

With your Savings Goals, use your Savings Goal Planner to work out how much you need to save each week/fortnight/month.

INCOME STREAMS

For the purpose of this budget workbook, we will work on a weekly budget. Whether you are paid weekly, fortnightly or monthly, please calculate each income stream to a weekly payment.
- Fortnightly income streams need to be multiplied by 26 then divided by 52.
- Monthly income streams need to be divided by 52.

INCOME STREAM	NETT INCOME (AFTER TAX)	PAYMENT FREQUENCY	AMOUNT PER WEEK

TOTAL WEEKLY INCOME

CASHFLOW QUADRANTS	AMOUNT
10% SAVINGS CASHFLOW	
10% SPLASH CASHFLOW	
10% DONATIONS CASHFLOW	
70% EXPENSE CASHFLOW	

EXPENSE CASHFLOW

To work out weekly amounts:

Fortnightly - multiply by 26 then divide by 52   Monthly - divide by 12

Quartlery - multiply by 4 then divide by 52   Yearly - divide by 52

EXPENSE DETAILS	AMOUNT	PAYMENT FREQUENCY	AMOUNT PER WEEK
GROCERIES			
Fruit & Vegetables			
Meat, Seafood, Deli			
Bakery			
Dairy, Eggs, Fridge			
Freezer			
Pantry			
Drinks			
Household			
Cleaning			
Baby			
Pets			
TOTAL WEEKLY GROCERIES EXPENSES			

EXPENSE CASHFLOW

To work out weekly amounts:

Fortnightly – multiply by 26 then divide by 52   Monthly – divide by 12
Quartlery – multiply by 4 then divide by 52   Yearly – divide by 52

EXPENSE DETAILS	AMOUNT	PAYMENT FREQUENCY	AMOUNT PER WEEK
RESIDENTIAL/UTILITIES			
Rent			
Mortgage			
Body Corporate Fees			
Council Rates			
Electricity			
Gas			
Water			
Internet			
Pay TV			
Subscriptions eg: Stan, Spotify etc			
Mobile Phone			
Landline Phone			
Furniture			
Appliances			
Linen/Curtains			
Carpet Cleaning			
Pest Control			
Lawn Maintenance			
Pool Maintenance			
TOTAL WEEKLY RESIDENTIAL/UTILITIES EXPENSES			

EXPENSE CASHFLOW

To work out weekly amounts:

Fortnightly - multiply by 26 then divide by 52   Monthly - divide by 12

Quartlery - multiply by 4 then divide by 52   Yearly - divide by 52

EXPENSE DETAILS	AMOUNT	PAYMENT FREQUENCY	AMOUNT PER WEEK
PERSONAL EXPENSES			
Sports/Gym			
Education			
Clothing, Shoes, Accessories			
Hairdresser/Barber			
Spa Treatments (Massage, Nails, Facial, etc)			
Skincare/Makeup Products			
Personal Care Products			
Medicine/Scripts			
Vitamins/Supplements			
Dental			
Eye Health (Glasses, Contact Lenses)			
Doctor			
Physiotherapy			
Counselling			
TOTAL WEEKLY PERSONAL EXPENSES			

EXPENSE CASHFLOW

To work out weekly amounts:

Fortnightly – multiply by 26 then divide by 52   Monthly – divide by 12
Quartlery – multiply by 4 then divide by 52   Yearly – divide by 52

EXPENSE DETAILS	AMOUNT	PAYMENT FREQUENCY	AMOUNT PER WEEK
VEHICLE/TRANSPORT			
Petrol/Gas/Diesel			
Tolls/Parking			
Car/Motorbike Registration			
Drivers Licence			
Roadside Assistance			
Car/Motorbike Servicing			
Car/Motorbike Tyres			
Boat Registration			
Public Transport			
Airfares			
Fines (I hope you don't have any)			
TOTAL WEEKLY VEHICLE/TRANSPORT EXPENSES			

EXPENSE CASHFLOW

To work out weekly amounts:

Fortnightly - multiply by 26 then divide by 52

Quartlery - multiply by 4 then divide by 52

Monthly - divide by 12

Yearly - divide by 52

EXPENSE DETAILS	AMOUNT	PAYMENT FREQUENCY	AMOUNT PER WEEK
FAMILY EXPENSES			
Baby/Toddler Products			
Childcare			
Babysitting			
School Fees			
School Uniforms			
School Books, Stationery			
School Excursions			
Child Support Payment			
Tuition			
Sporting Clubs			
Pets/Vets			
	TOTAL WEEKLY FAMILY EXPENSES		

EXPENSE CASHFLOW

To work out weekly amounts:

Fortnightly - multiply by 26 then divide by 52   Monthly - divide by 12
Quartlery - multiply by 4 then divide by 52   Yearly - divide by 52

EXPENSE DETAILS	AMOUNT	PAYMENT FREQUENCY	AMOUNT PER WEEK
ENTERTAINMENT & TREAT PURCHASES			
Coffee Shop			
Lunches			
Restaurants			
Take Away			
Menulog/Uber Eats etc			
Bars/Clubs			
Movies			
Concerts/Theatre			
Music			
Media Subscriptions eg: Magazine/Newspapers			
Books			
Jewellery & Accessories			
Birthday Gifts			
Christmas Gifts			
Other Gifts			
Hobbies/Crafts Products & Classes			
Technology (Computer, Tablet, Phone, Gadgets)			
Alcohol			
Cigarettes			
Gambling (Lotto, Art Union Tickets, etc)			
TOTAL WEEKLY ENTERTAINMENT & TREAT PURCHASES EXPENSES			

EXPENSE CASHFLOW

To work out weekly amounts:

Fortnightly - multiply by 26 then divide by 52

Quartlery - multiply by 4 then divide by 52

Monthly - divide by 12

Yearly - divide by 52

EXPENSE DETAILS	AMOUNT	PAYMENT FREQUENCY	AMOUNT PER WEEK
FINANCIAL & INSURANCES			
Car Insurance			
Motorbike Insurance			
Boat Insurance			
House Insurance			
Contents Insurance			
Private Health Insurance			
Life Insurance			
Superannuation			
Legal Fees			
Accounting			
Union & Professional Association Fees			
TOTAL WEEKLY FINANCIAL & INSURANCE EXPENSES			

EXPENSE CASHFLOW

To work out weekly amounts:

Fortnightly – multiply by 26 then divide by 52   Monthly – divide by 12
Quartlery – multiply by 4 then divide by 52   Yearly – divide by 52

EXPENSE DETAILS	AMOUNT	PAYMENT FREQUENCY	AMOUNT PER WEEK
LOANS / CREDIT CARDS / BNPL			
Mortgage			
Car Loan			
Credit Card #1			
Credit Card #2			
Credit Card #3			
AfterPay			
zipPay			
Other Buy Now Pay Later Accounts			
Student Loan			
TOTAL WEEKLY LOANS / CREDIT CARDS / BNPL EXPENSES			

TOTAL EXPENSES

To work out weekly amounts:

Fortnightly – multiply by 26 then divide by 52   Monthly – divide by 12
Quartlery – multiply by 4 then divide by 52   Yearly – divide by 52

EXPENSE DETAILS	AMOUNT PER WEEK
TOTAL WEEKLY GROCERIES EXPENSES	
TOTAL WEEKLY RESIDENTIAL/UTILITIES EXPENSES	
TOTAL WEEKLY PERSONAL EXPENSES	
TOTAL WEEKLY VEHICLE/TRANSPORT EXPENSES	
TOTAL WEEKLY FAMILY EXPENSES	
TOTAL WEEKLY ENTERTAINMENT & TREAT PURCHASES EXPENSES	
TOTAL WEEKLY FINANCIAL & INSURANCE EXPENSES	
TOTAL WEEKLY LOANS / CREDIT CARDS / BNPL EXPENSES	
TOTAL WEEKLY SAVING GOALS & OTHER EXPENSES	
TOTAL WEEKLY EXPENSES	

Now you have completed the expenses, you need to add each category.

Finally, it's time to work out if you are over or under budget and find out what your **EXCESS** is.

BUDGET BREAKDOWN

- To Calculate to Fortnightly – multiply weekly by 2
- To Calculate to Monthly – multiply weekly by 52 then divide by 12

EXPENSE DETAILS	WEEKLY	FORTNIGHTLY	MONTHLY
TOTAL AMOUNT REQUIRED FOR EXPENSES ENTER THE TOTAL WEEKLY EXPENSES FROM THE PREVIOUS PAGES.			
YOUR 70% EXPENSE CASHFLOW AVAILABLE ENTER YOUR WEEKLY 70% CASHFLOW FROM THE INCOME STREAMS.			
LESS YOUR CURRENT EXPENSES ENTER YOUR WEEKLY/FORTNIGHTLY/MONTHLY TOTAL AMOUNT REQUIRED FOR EXPENSES			
ARE YOU UNDER OR OVER BUDGET? CALCULATE YOUR 70% EXPENSE CASHFLOW LESS YOUR CURRENT EXPENSES			
MY BUDGET EXCESS IS:			

There is always room for improvement, so it is good to revisit your budget and cut back or research cheaper options.

JOURNAL

The following journal pages are here so you can record your 'aha' moments, thoughts and goals, and reflect on your progress.

Reading the information in this book is an important step, however, making your own notes helps you process the information in your own words.

Throughout your journey, revisit this book and journal to see how far you have come.

Journal / Notes

'Aha' Moments:

Journal / Notes

'Aha' Moments:

Journal / Notes

'Aha' Moments:

Journal / Notes

'Aha' Moments:

Journal / Notes

'Aha' Moments:

Journal / Notes

'Aha' Moments:

Journal / Notes

'Aha' Moments:

Journal / Notes

'Aha' Moments:

Journal / Notes

'Aha' Moments:

Journal / Notes

'Aha' Moments:

Journal / Notes

'Aha' Moments:

Journal / Notes

'Aha' Moments:

CONNECT WITH BUDGET RIGHT

Instagram: @budgetrightbook

Facebook: @budgetrightbook

YouTube: @budgetright

TikTok: @budgetright

Email: hello@budgetright.com.au

Website: www.budgetright.com.au

www.ingramcontent.com/pod-product-compliance
Lightning Source LLC
Chambersburg PA
CBHW052342210326
41597CB00037B/6231